The Second Big Book of
Afghans

The Second Big Book of
Afghans

by Valerie Kurita

A Genie Book

VAN NOSTRAND REINHOLD COMPANY
NEW YORK   CINCINNATI   TORONTO   LONDON   MELBOURNE

Book designed by Allan Mogel
Photography by Ernest Silva

Printed in the United States of America

Published by Van Nostrand Reinhold Company Inc.
135 West 50th Street, New York, NY 10020

Van Nostrand Reinhold Publishing
1410 Birchmount Road
Scarborough, Ontario M1P 2E7, Canada

Van Nostrand Reinhold Australia Pty. Ltd.
17 Queen Street
Mitcham, Victoria 3132, Australia

Van Nostrand Reinhold Company Limited
Molly Millars Lane
Wokingham, Berkshire, England

16 15 14 13 12 11 10 9 8 7 6 5 4 3 2 1

Library of Congress Cataloging in Publication Data

Kurita, Valerie.
    The second big book of afghans.

    Includes index.
    1. Afghans (Coverlets)   I. Title.
TT825.K86   746.9'7   82-6947
ISBN 0-442-24863-6   AACR2

ACKNOWLEDGMENTS

Special thanks go to the following professional craftswomen, whose effort and expertise made the creation of these thirty-six afghans possible.

Antonia Builes
Esther Schott
Jeannie Thibodeaux
Marjorie Williams
Bertha Zeltser

Thanks also go to Rita Quinn for her peerless typing and to Maggy Ramsay and Janet McEneaney for their careful direction checking.

* * *

The author would like to thank the following yarn companies for their courteous support and for the opportunity to work with their beautiful yarns. If your local yarn shop does not carry the yarn specified in the directions for our afghans, please write to the proper company below for purchasing and ordering information:

Coats & Clark Sales Corp.
  (Red Heart Yarn)
75 Rockefeller Plaza
New York, NY 10019

Phildar Inc.
6438 Dawson Blvd.
Norcross, GA 30093

Pingouin Yarns
9179 Red Ranch Road
Columbia, MD 21045

Reynolds Yarns, Inc.
15 Oser Avenue
Hauppauge, NY 11787

CONTENTS

Introduction/ 11
About the Book/ 13
Before You Begin/ 15
Metric Conversion Table and Standard Abbreviations/ 17

KNITTED AFGHANS

1/ **Seascape:** Knitted-in seagulls in their natural habitat/ 20
2/ **Log Cabin Quilt:** A traditional quilting pattern translated into simple garter-stitch squares/ 26
3/ **All Points:** Banners of beige, dark brown, and tweed stripe a handsome afghan/ 29
4/ **Irish Knit Updated:** Aran stitches utilized in a new way/ 31
5/ **Squares in the Round:** Brightly colored squares knitted with five double-pointed needles/ 35
6/ **Fan and Feather:** Traditional stitch in the nontraditional color combination of deep purple, gray, and black/ 37
7/ **Icelandic Accent:** Strips in honeycomb stitch and knit-in Icelandic design/ 39
8/ **Flowing Lace:** Gossamer-light and gold, it can even be worn as a shawl/ 42
9/ **Snowflakes:** Large snowflakes and light flurries on a powder blue background/ 44
10/ **Harlequin:** Bulky-knit diamonds alive with textured stitches and pom-poms/ 47
11/ **Chevron Stripes:** Soft rose and dusty green zigzag over a lovely afghan/ 49
12/ **Rattan:** Tropical tan stripes with jungle brown and sky gray-blue in a breezy, yarnover stitch/ 51

KNITTED LAP ROBES

13/ **Tiny Blossoms:** Soft, white mohair squares embroidered with pretty pink French-knot flowers/ 54
14/ **Arrowtip Lace:** Worked on large needles for an overall lacy effect/ 56
15/ **Argyle Borders:** Argyle breaks out of the socks-and-sweater mold, in gray, lilac, and yellow/ 58

KNITTED BABY BLANKETS

16/ **Ribbons and Bows:** A simple pointelle stitch beaded with yards of pastel ribbons/ 62
17/ **Patchwork Hearts:** Red, knit-in hearts on white squares alternate with white, knit-in hearts on red squares/ 66
18/ **Baby Smocking:** Baby blue ribbing embroidered with pink smocking stitch/ 70

CROCHETED AFGHANS

19/ Neon Granny: Shocking pink, turquoise, and yellow squares contrast with neon stripes on a black background/ 74

20/ Victorian Openwork: An old-fashioned effect, without the old-fashioned effort/ 77

21/ Woven Pastel Plaid: Misty lavender mohair woven through with lightest green and off-white/ 89

22/ Berry Stitch Get-Together: Raspberry pink squares of double crochet with berry-stitch designs at the intersections/ 93

23/ Flowers at the Crossroads: Green, textured crochet squares with brightly colored appliquéd bouquets/ 96

24/ Grapevines: Deep purple grapes grow from green vines on a black, crocheted background/ 99

25/ Lightning Strikes: Shaggy yarn in white flashes across a double-crochet background/ 102

26/ Parrot: A tropical bird is cross-stitched in bright colors on a sunny yellow afghan stitch/ 106

27/ Motifs Ahoy: Steering wheels in blue with life-preservers and twisted cord in white create a nautical mood/ 110

28/ Colonial Ripples: The perfect beginner's project in shades of autumn gold/ 114

29/ Blue Willow: Inspired by the famous china pattern—an embroidered scene on a delicately textured crocheted background/ 116

30/ Crayon Stripes: Bright stripes in double crochet with pinstripes of crisp, white single crochet/ 119

CROCHETED LAP ROBES

31/ Navajo Symbols: Authentic Navajo symbols in gray, black, and white/ 122

32/ Portable Lap Robe: Fold it up and carry it away by its own crocheted handles/ 126

33/ Stitch Sampler: Five different pattern stitches, some lacy, some solid, in a one-color lap robe/ 129

CROCHETED BABY BLANKETS

34/ Fiesta: Layer upon layer of bright orange, yellow, and blue ruffles with appliquéd balloons/ 134

35/ Pandas on Parade: Three big pandas frolic on bamboo-leaf green/ 137

36/ Baby's Bouquet: A large and lovely basket of cross-stitched violets to welcome baby/ 141

STITCH GLOSSARY/ 145

INDEX/ 168

INTRODUCTION

The making of knitted and crocheted afghans is one of the most popular project choices being made by needleworkers today. I can think of many reasons for this, but the best ones come from the hobbyists themselves. Among their comments are the following:

*In most cases, the small pieces that make up the whole can be carried along as portable handwork.

*An afghan doesn't go out of fashion (as a sweater might) before you've had a chance to complete it.

*There is a sense of creating an heirloom that will be passed on proudly from generation to generation.

*As a gift, there's no fear that it will be the wrong size, style, or color.

I think that this last point may be the most important of all because, more often than not, afghans, lap robes, and baby blankets are made for others rather than for oneself. An afghan can be given to anyone with the confidence that it will be regularly used because of the practical warmth it offers in these energy-saving days of lower indoor temperatures. Also, being on the receiving end of the afghan-as-gift gives one a cared-for feeling when one considers the time, effort, and skill expended on one's behalf by the maker.

So, here in response to popular demand, is a collection of new and unique designer afghans, lap robes, and baby blankets, utilizing a wide variety of yarns and techniques. There are projects for the beginner, intermediate, and expert handworker. I hope that those of you who start with the beginner projects, such as the knitted "All Points" or the crocheted "Colonial Ripples," will graduate to the intermediate and expert projects as you gain more confidence and skill. After all, an expert is only a beginner who kept trying something a little bit harder than what he or she just finished.

I think you'll enjoy the variety of the projects you can choose from. A new baby can be greeted by the appealing "Pandas on Parade" or "Patchwork Hearts." For sheer extravagance, what can match the lavender "Woven Pastel Plaid" or the gold "Flowing Lace," both made in a luxurious mohair? In the practicality department, the "Portable Lap Robe" is made with its own handles to be toted anywhere. Embroiderers will rejoice in the making of the tropical "Parrot," the delicate "Tiny Blossoms," and the Oriental "Blue Willow." For those addicted to granny squares, there's "Neon Granny," which is like no other granny-square afghan you've seen.

I wish you could reach out and touch all the projects photographed in this book, to experience the beautiful yarns and textures I've had the pleasure of working with. Now it's your turn to pick up yarn and needles or hook and create handmade treasures that you, your family, and friends will enjoy and cherish for a long time to come.

Now, please take a few minutes to read the next two sections, which explain "About the Book" and a few things you'll need to know "Before You Begin."

ABOUT THE BOOK

Simplified Instructions

In the fall of 1979, a committee of professionals from the yarn industry and many major consumer publications met to develop a simplified instruction system for handknitters and crocheters. This national committee standardized abbreviations and sizing to eliminate the confusion the handworker often encountered when following instructions from one publication to another. The standards the committee established have met with widespread acceptance throughout the United States. Whenever you see the "Simplified Instructions" logo (see p. 17), you can be assured that these standards have been complied with.

Instructions Format

At the beginning of each set of instructions given, you will note an "approximate finished size". Your finished project should work out to this size if you achieve the gauge listed in the instructions. (See "Before You Begin—Gauge," p. 15.)

When a project would be suitable for a beginner, the designation "No Experience Needed" is given. Likewise "Experienced Crocheters or Knitters Only" indicates that a more advanced degree of skill is needed. The remaining projects have no designation and are for the average handworker.

A black and white photograph accompanies each set of directions to show stitch details, the positioning of components, and anything crucial to the design of the project. Underneath the photos, you'll find alternate color suggestions or uses for the project, such as for wall hangings or rugs.

Four yarn companies have generously supplied their beautiful yarns to make many of the projects in this book. For the best results, use the yarns specified (see "Acknowledgments" for company addresses). Under "Materials," the brand name, number, and name of each color and the amount of each yarn required have been listed. However, should you desire to substitute a different yarn, refer to the generic yarn type that appears in parentheses (sport weight, knitting worsted weight, bulky weight, or mohair-type), making sure that your yarn matches the gauge specified in the directions as closely as possible and that the total amount, in weight, that you buy equals the amount specified. Whenever the name of a color might not be easily understood and substituted for, an explanation follows in parentheses.

Following the directions given for each project, you'll find a "Handwork Hints" section. A few sentences detailing the finer points to keep in mind when following the instructions will help you produce, more easily, a beautifully finished piece. These hints will also come in handy for future projects.

Stitch Glossary

All the basic knit, crochet, embroidery, and joining stitches used in the projects are clearly described here with accompanying illustrations. They are, however, no substitute for a "hands-on" teacher. So, try to find an experienced (and patient) friend, relative, or yarn-shop owner who can demonstrate unfamiliar stitches to you.

BEFORE YOU BEGIN

About Gauge

Gauge is the all-important word that determines the texture and finished size of your project. To save time in the long run, take the time to check the gauge by working a test piece of at least 4 inches. For example, with a gauge in stockinette stitch (St st) of 5 stitches = 1 inch; 7 rows = 1 inch, work a test piece as follows:

TEST PIECE: Cast on 20 sts. Work in St st for 28 rows. Piece should measure 4 inches square. If too small, try larger needles; if too large, try smaller needles, until correct gauge is obtained.

Reading Charts

When reading the charts in this book, start at the bottom, reading the odd-numbered rows from right to left and the even-numbered rows from left to right. Usually, unless otherwise specified, the odd-numbered row will be a right-side row and the even-numbered row will be a wrong-side row. If all the rows are not shown on the chart, it will be specified as such in the directions.

Working Single-Crocheted Edgings

Often the directions will call for a single-crocheted edging to be worked around each component or around the entire joined piece. It will usually be up to you to determine the number of stitches needed for the work to lie flat.

For instance, if you work across the edge of a knitted square, working one single crochet into each stitch, you may find that the edge is too stretched-out. In that case, rip back and try another system, such as skipping every third stitch, until you are satisfied that the edge will be the proper size. Once this is established, be absolutely certain that you work the same number of stitches along each side of the square with three stitches worked into the center stitch of each corner. In most cases, it's best to work the edging so that it seems a tiny bit tight because when it is stretched or blocked, it will flatten out to just the right size. When working along the edge of a knitted piece, you will usually observe a knot followed by a long thread, then another knot followed by a long thread, and so forth. Whenever possible, work the single-crochet stitch into the knot rather than the thread, thereby eliminating the formation of a series of holes along the finished edge.

Working Color over Color

The directions may ask you to work a single-crocheted edging color over color or a row of fringe color over color. This means that you match the color of the edging or fringe to the color on the edge of the main piece.

Seaming

The best way to ensure nearly invisible seams is to use an overcast or running back stitch (see Stitch Glossary) on the wrong side of the work, matching stitch to stitch so that the patterns match and the work lies flat.

Blocking

Some materials, such as mohair, should never be blocked, and many of the best new yarns need little or no blocking. Blocking will be specified in the directions only when it is absolutely crucial to the work. For instance, when squares are knitted on the diagonal, they often appear diamond-shaped and must first be blocked before they can be properly edged and joined. In this case, pin the piece, in the desired shape, to a padded board and steam with an iron over a damp towel, never putting full pressure on the towel but rather allowing the steam to do the work. Do not remove the pieces until they are completely dry. In all other cases, you be the judge, keeping in mind the yarn type and whether or not the seams or pieces of your knitted or crocheted work need blocking to achieve a finished look.

Fringing

To knot fringe, insert a crochet hook from back to front through the stitch to be fringed, catch the middle of the group of fringe strands with the hook, and pull it partly through the stitch, making a loop. Catch all ends of the strands with the hook and pull them through the loop. Pull the ends to tighten the knot.

METRIC CONVERSION TABLE

Linear Measure:

1 inch = 2.54 centimeters
12 inches = 1 foot = 0.3048 meter
3 feet = 1 yard = 0.9144 meter

Square Measure:

1 square inch = 6.451 square centimeters
144 square inches = 1 square foot = 929.03 square centimeters
9 square feet = 1 square yard = 0.8361 square meter

ABBREVIATIONS

beg	begin(ning)
CC	contrasting color
ch	chain
ch-	(chain dash) refers to chain or space previously made, e.g., ch-1 sp
dc	double crochet
dec	decrease, decreases, decreased, decreasing
dp	double point
hdc	half double crochet
inc	increase, increases, increased, increasing
k	knit
lp(s)	loop(s)
MC	main color
p	purl
pat(s)	pattern(s)
psso	pass slip stitch(es) over [stitch(es)]
rem	remain(ing)
rep	repeat
rnd(s)	round(s)
sc	single crochet
SKP	slip 1, knit 1, pass slip stitch(es) over knit stitch(es)
sl st	slip stitch
sp(s)	space(s)
St st	stockinette st
st(s)	stitch(es)
tog	together
tr	triple crochet
yo	yarn over

Simplified Instructions

KNITTED AFGHANS

₁ **Seascape**

Approximate finished size: 55 by 60 inches

Sand, sea, and sky—the natural habitat of knit-in white seagulls in stockinette stitch. Three strips of broad knit-in color areas are worked by following three separate coordinating charts. After the strips have been joined, the details on the seagulls are filled in with simple embroidery. This could make a beautiful wall hanging for a beach house by eliminating the fringe and backing the piece with a sturdy canvas.

Materials:
Pingouin Pingoland, 50-gram (1¾-ounce) balls (bulky weight)
    17 balls color 803, porcelaine (light blue)
     4 balls color 843, bleu roy (navy blue)
     3 balls color 801, blanc (white)
     1 ball color 831, feu (red)
Pingouin Iceberg, 50-gram (1¾-ounce) balls (bulky weight)
    10 balls color 99, chameau (tan)
Knitting needles, No. 10½
Crochet hook, size H
Yarn needle

Gauge: 8 stitches = 3 inches; 4 rows = 1 inch

Note: Each row on chart is a knit row. Color changes are worked on knit rows only. For each purl row, simply knit the colors in the sequence established on the previous knit row (purl the red stitches in red, blue in blue, etc.).

Strips: For each strip, cast on 49 sts with tan and work even in St st (k 1 row, p 1 row) throughout. Make one strip of each of the three different charts, working the 240 rows of each to completion. Bind off.

Finishing: Sew strips tog on wrong side of work with a running back st (see Stitch Glossary), working color over color. Work 1 row of sc around outside edge of joined piece, color over color, working 3 sc in each corner.

Fringe: Cut 14-inch strands of yarn and knot 3 strands in every third st around, color over color.

Embroidery: Refer to the embroidery charts, which show the seagull from each of the three strips as each appears when the knitting is completed. Both k and p rows are shown on them. Embroider the duplicate stitch (see Stitch Glossary), as indicated, around each seagull. Fill in the outlines of the seagull of Chart 1, using long satin stitches for the tail feathers and long and short stitches for the head and body (see Stitch Glossary).

☞ **Handwork Hints:** Use separate balls of the same color yarn when it must be carried over more than 4 or 5 stitches. In this way, long threads on the wrong side of the work are eliminated and yarn waste is kept to a minimum. To make following the charts easier, make a Xerox or photocopy of them and use a ruler, a pin, or one of the handy metal clipboards with magnetic strips to help you keep your place.

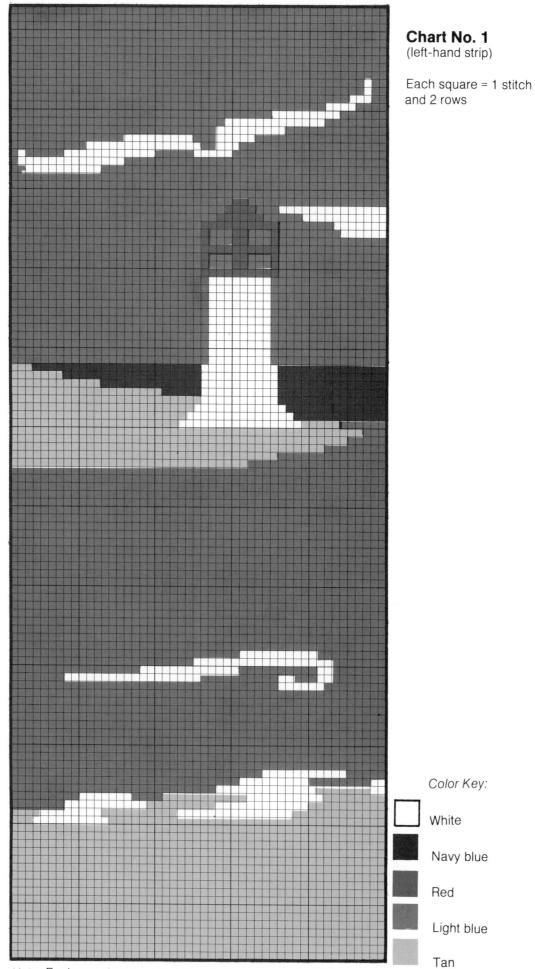

Chart No. 1
(left-hand strip)

Each square = 1 stitch
and 2 rows

Color Key:

White

Navy blue

Red

Light blue

Tan

22

Note: Each row shown on chart is a knit row (see also Note in text).

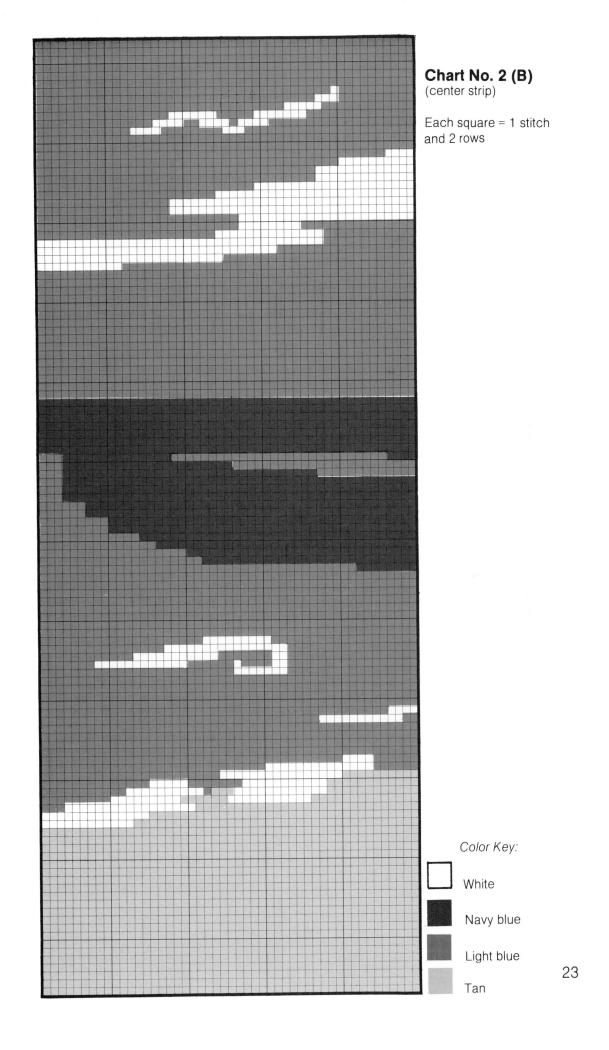

Chart No. 2 (B)
(center strip)

Each square = 1 stitch
and 2 rows

Color Key:

☐ White

■ Navy blue

■ Light blue

■ Tan

23

Chart No. 3
(right-hand strip)

Each square = 1 stitch
and 2 rows

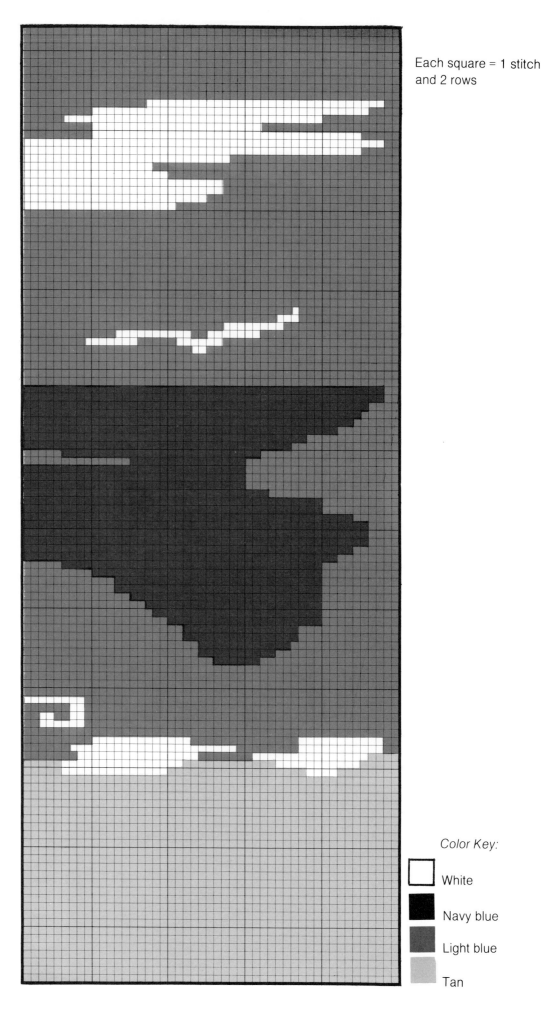

Color Key:

White

Navy blue

Light blue

Tan

24

Seagull from Chart No. 1

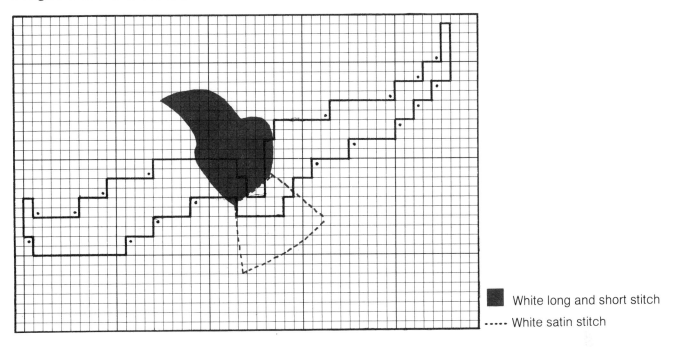

White long and short stitch
----- White satin stitch

Seagull from Chart No. 2

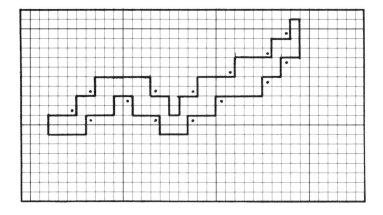

Embroidery Charts

Embroidery Key:
- = White duplicate stitch

Each square = 1 stitch and 1 row

Seagull from Chart No. 3

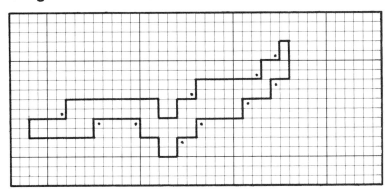

²Log Cabin Quilt

Approximate finished size: 50 by 54 inches

For this afghan, the traditional log-cabin quilting pattern has been translated into twenty, simple garter-stitch squares done in two tones of blue, pink, and dark rose. If you wish to make coordinating pillows, follow the directions for Square D so that the navy blue borders all four edges. To make a dramatic wall hanging of this blanket, reinforce the edges by sewing wide rug binding on the wrong side of the work and then tack the edges to stretcher bars.

Materials:
Pingouin Pingoland, 50-gram (1¾-ounce) balls (bulky weight)
    13 balls color 843, bleu roy (navy blue)
    10 balls color 834, dragée (light pink)
    10 balls color 803, porcelaine (powder blue)
     9 balls color 823, éveque (dark rose)
Knitting needles, No. 11
Yarn needle

Gauge: 8 stitches = 3 inches; 5 rows = 1 inch

Pattern Stitch: Work in garter st (k every row) throughout.

Square A: Make 12. With navy blue, cast on 32 sts. Following chart for number of rows to be worked and color changes, work to completion. Bind off.

Square B: Make 4. With navy blue, cast on 38 sts. Following chart for number of rows to be worked and color changes, work to completion. Bind off.

Square C: Make 3. With navy blue, cast on 32 sts. Following chart for number of rows to be worked and color changes, work to completion. Bind off.

Square D: Make 1. With navy blue, cast on 38 sts. Following chart for number of rows to be worked and color changes, work to completion. Bind off.

Finishing: Following the placement diagram, sew the squares tog on the wrong side of the work with an overcast st (see Stitch Glossary), being careful not to pull the sts too tightly as you go.

☞ **Handwork Hints:** Since each of the squares here have vertical stripes, careful changing of yarn color is necessary to prevent leaving gaps in the work. When you wish to change, have the old color on the wrong side of the work, hold it to the left, and bring the new color up from underneath. This technique twists the yarn, so that there will be no holes in the work. On Squares B and D, after the first 6 rows have been completed, work the 6 stitches on the right edge of the square with a separate ball of navy blue to avoid having to carry the yarn across the back of the square.

Placement Diagram

C	C	C	D
A	A	A	B
A	A	A	B
A	A	A	B
A	A	A	B

Stitch and Color Chart

End here as indicated for each square

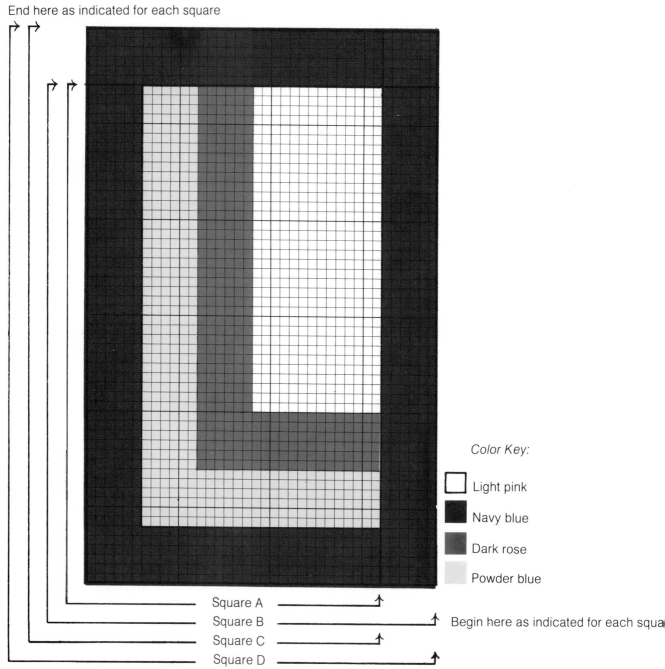

Color Key:

☐ Light pink

■ Navy blue

■ Dark rose

■ Powder blue

Square A ⟶

Square B ⟶   Begin here as indicated for each squa

Square C ⟶

Square D ⟶

³ All Points

Approximate finished size: 61 by 64 inches

No Experience Needed

Long, narrow strips pointed at each end are knitted in simple stockinette stitch using bulky yarns in beige, dark brown, and tweed. After the strips have been sewn together, a heavy tassel in a matching color is added to accentuate each point.

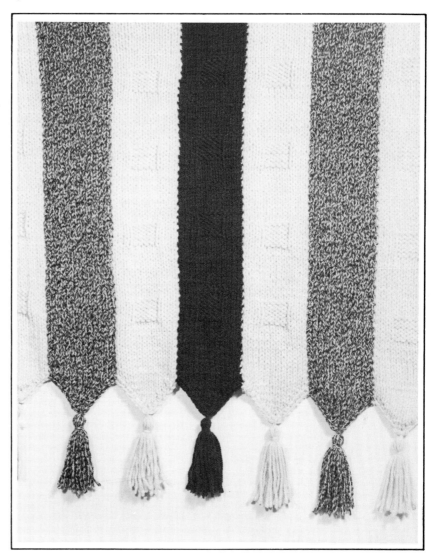

Materials:
Phildar Kadischa, 50-gram (1¾-ounce) balls (bulky weight)
    18 balls color 172, mouette (beige)
     9 balls color 134, cayenne (tweed)
     6 balls color 150, tabou (dark brown)
Knitting needles, No. 11
Crochet hook, size J
Yarn needle

Gauge: 7 stitches = 3 inches; 10 rows = 3 inches

Strip No. 1: Make 6. With beige, cast on 3 sts. Working in St st (k 1 row, p 1 row), inc 1 st at beg and end of every other row until there are 13 sts. *Work even in St st for 14 rows. Box: (*Next Row:* K 4, p 5, k 4; *Next Row:* P 4, k 5, p 4) 3 times. Repeat from * 8 times more and end 14 rows St st. Working in St st, dec 1 st at beg and end of every other row until there are 3 sts remaining. Bind off.

Strip No. 2: Make 2. With dark brown, work as for Strip No. 1.

Strip No. 3: Make 3. With tweed, work as for Strip No. 1, but work in St st only throughout, eliminating the 6-row box and being sure to work the same total number of rows as the other strips.

Finishing: Sew strips tog with overcast or running back st (see Stitch Glossary) on wrong side of work, being careful to match rows and positioning the strips from left to right by number as follows: (Strip No. 1, No. 3, No. 1, No. 2) twice, ending No. 1, No. 3, No. 1. Work 1 row of sc, color over color, around entire joined piece, working 3 sc in each corner and each point.

Tassels: Make 12 beige, 4 dark brown, and 6 tweed. For each tassel, cut sixteen 10-inch strands of yarn and tie a 7-inch strand around the middle. Fold the strands in half at the tie, wrap one end of one of the strands securely around the folded strands 1 inch below the tie, fasten off, and trim the ends evenly. Tie one tassel to each point on a matching color strip. Block the seams.

☞ **Handwork Hints:** When working the single-crochet edging around the points of each strip, you will notice that the points with the increase stitches have holes along the edges. Eliminate these holes, making a firm, neat edge, by working the single-crochet stitch not into the hole or into the knit stitch on the very outside edge, but rather into the knit stitch after the hole created by the increase stitch.

④ Irish Knit Updated

Approximate finished size: 44 by 60 inches

Experienced Knitters Only

Off-white squares, knitted on the diagonal, utilize the traditional techniques of Irish knit—popcorns, cables, and seed stitch. When joined, they combine in a unique manner that has a contemporary look, with thick crocheted chains, tassels, and fringe adding an extra dimension. Perfect finishing is the key to success in this "experts only" afghan. For a matching pillow, make four more squares, join them in the same manner as the afghan, back the piece with off-white linen, and stuff. Trim the edge with the same heavy crocheted chain and add a tassel to the center and one at each corner.

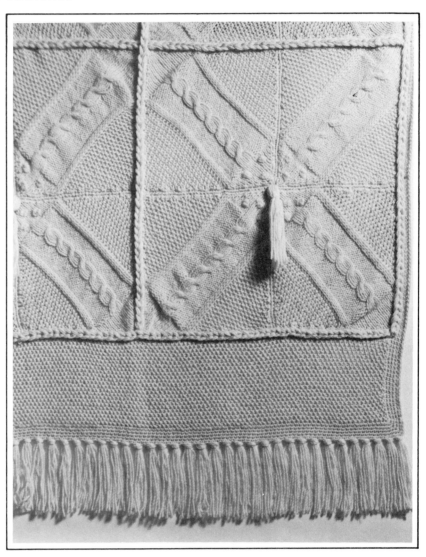

Materials:
Reynolds Portuguese Fisherman (Scoured), 100-gram (3.5-ounce) skeins (knitting worsted weight)
    13 skeins off-white
Knitting needles, No. 10
Crochet hooks, sizes G and J
Yarn needle

Gauge in Stockinette Stitch: 7 stitches = 2 inches; 11 rows = 2 inches

Cable Stitch: Sl 2 sts onto dp needle and hold at back of work, k 2 sts from left-hand needle, k 2 sts from dp needle—cable completed.

Popcorn Stitch:
Row 1: In next 2 sts tog, work (k 1, p 1, k 1, p 1). Turn work to wrong side.
Row 2: P 4. Turn work to right side.
Row 3: K 4. Turn work.
Row 4: (P 2 tog) twice. Turn work.
Row 5: K 2—popcorn completed.

Note: Chart shows only right-side rows. On wrong-side rows, work each st as it appears (k the k sts, p the p sts) except on seed-st section—k those that appear as p sts, p those that appear as k sts.

Squares: Make 16. Cast on 2 sts. Work in St st (k 1 row, p 1 row) for 16 rows, inc 1 st at beg and end of every right-side row (18 sts). Continuing to inc 1 st at beg and end of each right-side row, follow chart for st pat until there are 48 sts. Now dec 1 st at beg and end of each right-side row, follow chart to completion—2 sts remaining. Bind off. (Each square should measure approximately 10½ inches when blocked.)

Strips: Make 2. Cast on 25 sts.
Row 1: *K 1, p 1, rep from * across, end k 1. Rep Row 1 until strip measures the same as the length of four squares joined tog (approximately 42 inches). Bind off.

Finishing: Adjust squares on a padded surface so that they measure 10½ inches on each side and pin in place. Steam with a wet cloth and allow to dry in place. Remove pins and work 1 row of sc around each blocked square, working 3 sc in each corner. Sew the squares together with an overcast st (see Stitch Glossary) on right side of work, arranging them in four 4-square groups so that the popcorn-st corners meet in the center of each group. Now sew the four 4-square groups together to form one large square. Sew one 42-inch strip along one edge of the square and the remaining strip along

Irish Knit Square Chart

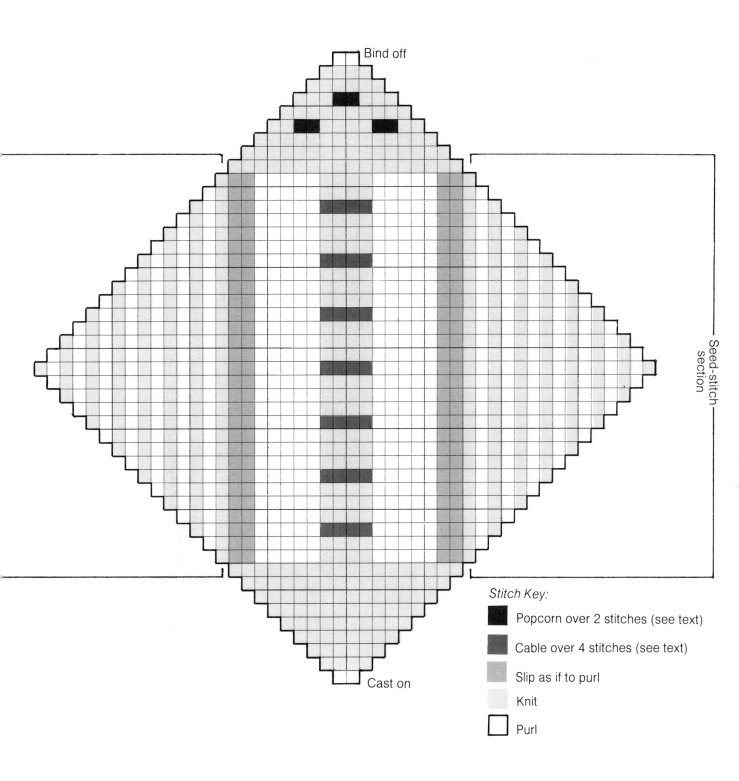

Bind off

Cast on

Seed-stitch section

Stitch Key:

▪ Popcorn over 2 stitches (see text)

▪ Cable over 4 stitches (see text)

▪ Slip as if to purl

▫ Knit

☐ Purl

the opposite edge. With G hook, work 5 rows of sc around the outside of the entire joined piece, working 3 sc in each of the four corners.

Chain Trim: With J hook and four strands of yarn, crochet two chains long enough to cover the two center seams between the four 4-square groups (about 42 inches) and one long enough to fit around the entire outside edge of the large square. Sew in place.

Tassels: Make 4. Cut twenty 14-inch strands of yarn and tie around the center with a 7-inch strand. Fold the strands in half at the tie, wrap one end of one of the strands securely around the folded strands 1 inch below the tie, fasten off, and trim the ends evenly. Sew one tassel in the center of each of the four-square groups.

Fringe: Cut 13-inch lengths of yarn and knot 4 strands in every third st along the two short ends of the blanket. Trim ends evenly.

☞ **Handwork Hints:** Usually blocking is done with a damp cloth. Blocking a diamond-shaped piece into a square, as we do in this project, however, requires a soaking wet cloth. Do not press down with the iron; the steam will do the work. If you allow the piece to dry completely before removing the pins and have been careful to work the same number of single crochet along each side of the piece, the result will be a perfect square.

⑤ Squares in the Round

Approximate finished size: 50 by 62 inches

Squares striped in pink, yellow, green, and blue, each knitted on four double-pointed needles from the outside in toward the center, are joined to form a striking pattern. A broad, single-crocheted edge frames the knitted squares.

Materials:
Pingouin Pingochamp, 100-gram (3.5-ounce) skeins (knitting worsted weight)
> 5 skeins color 313, fuchsia (pink)
> 3 skeins color 358, bright green
> 3 skeins color 304, lemon frost (yellow)
> 3 skeins color 349, royal blue

Five double-pointed (dp) knitting needles, No. 10
Crochet hook, size G
Yarn needle

Gauge in Stockinette Stitch: 11 stitches = 3 inches; 16 rows = 3 inches; each square = approximately 12 inches

Note: Each square is worked in rnds. Be careful not to twist the cast-on sts when working from one needle to the next.

Squares: Make 20. With pink, cast on 51 sts on each of 4 dp needles (204 sts).
Rnd 1: With pink, k, working dec rnd across 51 sts on each of the four needles as follows: SKP, k to within last 2 sts, k 2 tog.
Rnd 2: P.
Rep last 2 rnds 3 times more, working next 2 rnds with blue, next 2 rnds with yellow, and next 2 rnds with green. Now, k every row, working each rnd as a dec rnd (see Rnd 1) in color sequence as follows: 4 rnds pink, 4 rnds blue, 4 rnds yellow, 4 rnds green, and then continuing with pink until 3 sts remain on each needle.
Next Rnd: Continuing with pink, work dec at beg only of each needle (2 sts left on each needle).
Next Rnd: K 2 tog on each needle.
Next Rnd: K each st on each needle. Cut yarn and pull through remaining 4 sts. Fasten off.

Finishing: Block each square, on the wrong side of the work, to approximately 12 inches. Sew squares tog, four squares wide by five squares long, using overcast st (see Stitch Glossary) on right side of work. With pink, work 3 rnds of sc around the outside edge of the joined piece, working 3 sc in each corner. Block finished piece if necessary.

☞ **Handwork Hints:** To maintain flexibility at the corners of the squares for neater blocking, work the decrease stitches at the beginning and end of each needle loosely.

⑥ Fan and Feather

Approximate finished size: 48 by 60 inches

No afghan collection can be considered complete without the inclusion of a piece done in the traditional fan-and-feather pattern. This one is worked in deep purple, gray, and black, and it has been left untrimmed, although you might like to embellish yours with purple tassels attached to the center of each "fan" at the top and bottom edges.

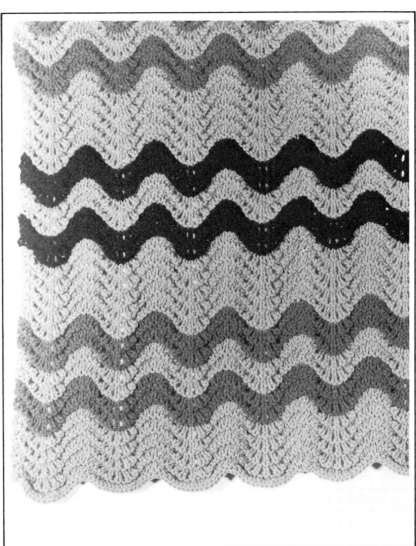

Materials:
Knitting worsted, 3.5-ounce skeins
    7 skeins gray (A)
    2 skeins purple (B)
    2 skeins black (C)
Knitting needles, No. 9
Yarn needle

Gauge in Pattern Stitch: 9 stitches = 2 inches

Pattern Stitch:
Rows 1 and 4: K.
Row 2: P.
Row 3: (K 2 tog) 3 times, *(yo, k 1) 6 times, (k 2 tog) 6 times, rep from * across, ending last rep with (k 2 tog) 3 times instead of 6 times. Rep Rows 1 through 4 for pat st.

Strips: Make 3. With A, cast on 72 sts. Work in pat st and color sequence as follows: (20 rows A, 8 rows B, 8 rows A, 8 rows B, 20 rows A, 8 rows C, 8 rows A, 8 rows C) 3 times, ending 20 rows A, 8 rows B, 8 rows A, 8 rows B, 20 rows A. Bind off.

Finishing: Sew the strips tog with an overcast st (see Stitch Glossary) on the wrong side of the work, working color over color.

☞ **Handwork Hints:** The key to sewing these strips together invisibly is to match row to row when working the overcast stitch, checking the right side of the work as you go and stretching the seams every few stitches to maintain the same tension as the knitted piece.

Icelandic Accent

Approximate finished size: 52 by 56 inches

The multicolor design on the light-colored strips of this Icelandic-style afghan is worked with a special slip-stitch technique so that only one color is used on each row, which greatly simplifies the color-changing procedure. The honeycomb stitch on the dark brown strips is also speeded along through the use of slip stitches. The result is a richly textured blanket that looks complicated but is actually so simple that anyone who has mastered the basics of knitting should try it—a little practice with the techniques to be used is all that's necessary. Although the homespun type of yarn recommended is very warm, it works up into a surprisingly lightweight cover.

Materials:

Reynolds Icelandic Homespun, 1¾-ounce balls (knitting worsted weight)

> 11 balls color 410, dark brown
> 6 balls color 401, off-white
> 1 ball color 406, gray

Knitting needles, No. 10

Crochet hook, size G

Yarn needle

Gauge in Stockinette Stitch: 7 stitches = 2 inches; 6 rows = 1 inch

Note: K all odd-numbered rows of chart; p all even-numbered rows. Also, be sure to read the "Handwork Hints" before starting.

Charted Strips: Make 3. With off-white, cast on 25 sts. Work even for 6 rows in St st (k 1 row, p 1 row), *work 40-row chart to completion, work 10½ inches even in off-white St st, rep from * twice more, work 40-row chart once more, and end 6 rows St st in off-white. Bind off.

Honeycomb-Stitch Strips: Make 4. With dark brown, cast on 33 sts.

Rows 1, 3, 5, and 7 (wrong side): P.

Row 2: K 1, *carrying yarn in front of work, sl 3 sts as if to p, k 1, rep from * across.

Row 4: K 2, *pick up yarn and k tog with next st, k 3, rep from * across, ending pick up yarn and k tog with next st, k 2.

Row 6: K 3, *carrying yarn in front of work, sl 3 sts as if to p, k 1, rep from * across, ending k 2.

Row 8: K 4, *pick up yarn and k tog with next st, k 3, rep from * across, ending k 1.

Rep Rows 1 through 8 until piece measures same as charted strips (approximately 56 inches). Bind off.

Finishing: Sew strips tog on wrong side of work with running back st (see Stitch Glossary), positioning one honeycomb strip at each outside edge with charted strips and remaining honeycomb strips alternating between. Work 1 row of sc, color over color, around the outside edge of joined piece.

Fringe: Cut 9-inch lengths of dark brown and off-white yarn. Knot 6 strands, color over color, in every other st along top and bottom edges of afghan.

☞ **Handwork Hints:** To save time, you will find when working the chart that you don't need to slip all stitches to the end of the row when only a few stitches are worked in one color in the center of the row (such as Row 7)—simply

turn the work when you reach the last sl st indicated on
the chart. Before starting to work the strip, be sure to
practice the color-changing techniques on the chart until
you are familiar with them.

Icelandic Accent Chart

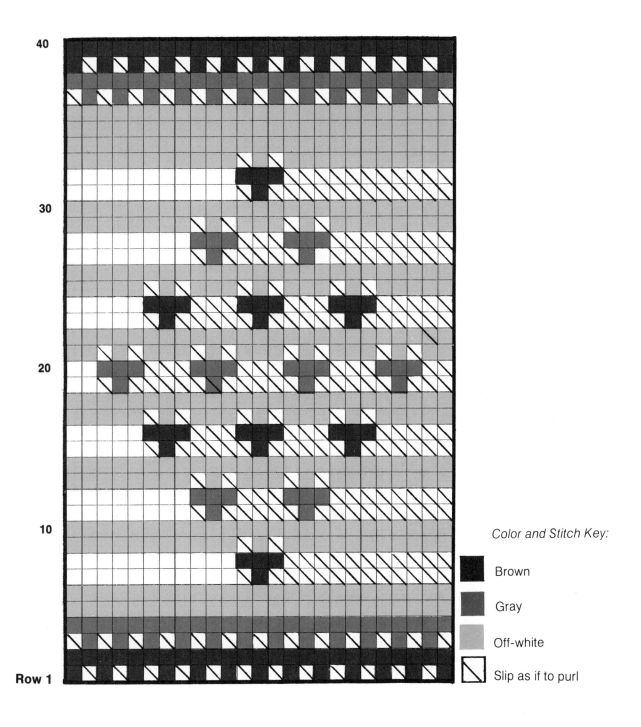

Color and Stitch Key:

Brown

Gray

Off-white

Slip as if to purl

⑧ Flowing Lace

Approximate finished size: 60 by 60 inches

Knitted in three separate strips on large needles, this gold mohair afghan is gossamer-light and trimmed with 8-strand fringes. Perfect for evenings when just a light cover is needed, it can even be folded double into a triangle and worn as a dramatic shawl.

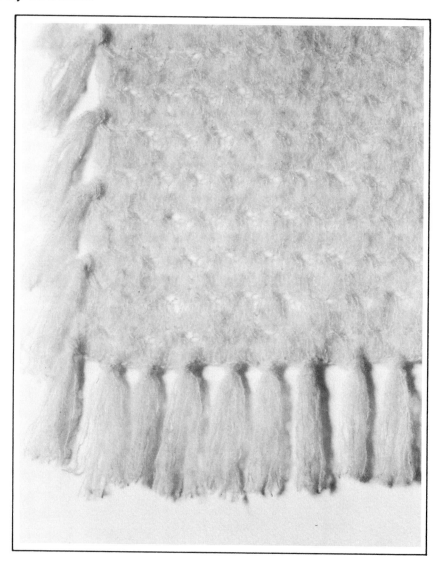

Materials:
Pingouin Laine et Mohair, 50-gram (1¾-ounce) balls (medium-weight mohair)
    16 balls color 09, soleil (gold)
Knitting needles, No. 10½
Crochet hook, size G
Yarn needle

Gauge in Pattern Stitch: 17 stitches = 5 inches

Strips: Make 3. Cast on 67 sts loosely.
Row 1: K 2, *yo, k 1, rep from * across, ending yo, k 3.
Row 2: P 3, *drop yo, p 1, rep from * across, ending drop yo, p 2.
Row 3: K 1, *sl 2 sts, k 2 tog, pass 2 sl sts over k 2 tog st, (k 1 through front lp, k 1 through back lp) twice in next st, rep from * across, ending k 1.
Row 4: P.
Row 5: Work as for Row 1.
Row 6: Work as for Row 2.
Row 7: K 1, *(k 1 through front lp, k 1 through back lp) twice in next st, sl 2, k 2 tog, pass 2 sl sts over k 2 tog st, rep from * across, ending k 1.
Row 8: P.
Rep Rows 1 through 8 for pat st. Work even until strip measures 60 inches from beg. Bind off loosely.

Finishing: Sew strips tog on wrong side of work with an overcast st (see Stitch Glossary), being careful not to pull sts too tightly. Work 1 row of sc around outside edge of piece, working 3 sc in each corner.

Fringe: Cut 12-inch strands of yarn and knot 8 strands in every fifth st around.

☞ **Handwork Hints:** Practice the 8 rows of pattern stitch on 17 stitches until you have the order of the stitches and the gauge well established. With this type of pattern stitch, which involves yarnovers, the working tension varies greatly from worker to worker. Don't be surprised if you require needles one to two sizes different from the ones specified here. Also, since the finished size is not crucial, you may decide upon a gauge that produces smaller or larger holes, for a tighter-knit or more lacy effect, as desired.

Snowflakes

Approximate finished size: 45 by 56 inches

A snowstorm of large, knitted-in, white snowflakes at each short end of this soft, powder blue afghan thins to light flurries of tiny flakes toward the center. Knitted in strips and fringed at two ends, it makes a snuggly warmer with a Scandinavian touch. The unembroidered solid blue center of the three strips making up the afghan can be worked longer or shorter for a custom-made length, and an extra strip can be added to make it blanket-size, if you wish. The white embroidered duplicate stitch can be continued for additional rows if an overall snowflake effect is desired.

Materials:
Reynolds Icelandic Homespun, 50-gram (1¾-ounce) balls
(knitting worsted weight)
    9 balls color 419, powder blue
    2 balls color 401, off-white
Knitting needles, No. 10
Crochet hook, size G
Yarn needle

Gauge: 10 stitches = 3 inches; 5 rows = 1 inch

Strips: Make 3. Work in St st (k 1 row, p 1 row) throughout. With powder blue, cast on 50 sts. Work 6 rows even. Change to off-white, and work 2 rows even. Change to powder blue, work 2 rows even. Work the 31-row snowflake chart to completion. Work even in powder blue for 39 inches. Work the 31 rows of the snowflake chart in reverse, ending with 2 rows powder blue, 2 rows off-white, 6 rows powder blue. Bind off.

Finishing: Sew strips tog with running back st (see Stitch Glossary) on wrong side of work. With powder blue, work 1 row of sc around joined piece, working 3 sc in each corner. Work 1 row of reverse sc along two long sides (work as for sc but work from left to right instead of right to left). Carry out the off-white snowflake pat in duplicate st (see Stitch Glossary) as shown on chart.

Fringe: Cut 9-inch lengths of powder blue yarn and knot 3 strands in every other st at top and bottom of afghan.

☞ **Handwork Hints:** When working the large snowflakes on the chart, use a separate ball of off-white for each snowflake to avoid having to carry long strands across the back of the work.

Snowflake Chart

Color and Stitch Key:

▢ Powder blue

◼ White stockinette stitch

▩ White duplicate stitch (work after strips are completed and joined)

Harlequin

Approximate finished size: 48 by 57 inches, at widest and longest points

No Experience Needed

Made in bulky camel yarn, this afghan is accented by earthtone pom-poms. Seed-stitch and stockinette-stitch diamonds alternate for variety of texture. If you're ambitious, you can easily increase the number of diamonds to make a beautiful double bedspread.

Materials:
Pingouin Pingoland, 50-gram (1¾-ounce) balls (bulky weight)
22 balls color 817, camel
3 balls color 853, ecru
3 balls color 848, chocolat
Knitting needles, No. 10½
Crochet hook, size J
Yarn needle

Gauge: 11 stitches = 5 inches; 10 rows = 3 inches

Note: Work stockinette-stitch and seed-stitch diamonds in camel.

Seed-Stitch Pattern:
Row 1: K 1, *p 1, k 1, rep from * across.
Row 2: Rep Row 1, positioning the k sts over those that appear as p sts and the p sts over those that appear as k sts.

Stockinette-Stitch Diamonds: Make 9. Cast on 3 sts. Inc 1 st at beg and end of first and every other row until there are 33 sts, working in St st (k 1 row, p 1 row) throughout. Work 1 row even. Dec 1 st at beg and end of next and every other row until 3 sts remain. Bind off.

Seed-Stitch Diamonds: Make 4. Work shaping as for St-st diamonds, but work in seed-st pat throughout, being sure to work inc sts into pat.

Finishing: Work 1 row of sc around each diamond, working 3 sc in each corner. Sew diamonds tog on wrong side of work with an overcast st (see Stitch Glossary and "Handwork Hints" on p. 98), placing (3 St-st diamonds on first row, 2 seed-st diamonds on the next row) twice, ending with a row of 3 St-st diamonds (see photo). Work 1 row of sc around entire joined piece, working 3 sc into each point.

Tassels: Make 12. Cut twenty 10-inch strands of camel yarn for each tassel and tie with a 7-inch strand around the middle. Fold the strands in half at the tie, wrap one end of one of the strands securely around the folded strands 1 inch below the tie, fasten off, and trim the ends evenly. Tie one tassel to each point around the outside edge of the blanket.

Pom-poms: Make 4 in ecru, 5 in chocolat. For each pom-pom, wind the yarn 45 times around a 4-inch-square piece of cardboard. Remove the yarn from the cardboard and tie it in the middle with a separate 7-inch strand of matching yarn. Cut the loops at each end and fluff out the pom-pom. Trim the ends evenly and sew to the St-st squares, alternating colors as shown in the photo.

¹¹ Chevron Stripes

Approximate finished size: 40 by 60 inches

No Experience Needed

Knitted in two separate strips, this afghan is of soft rose and a dusty green and utilizes a stitch that creates the look of chevron stripes in a simple way.

Materials:
Phildar Leader 010, 100-gram (3.5-ounce) balls (knitting worsted weight)
    5 balls color 03, opaline green
    3 balls color 05, empire rose
Knitting needles, No. 10
Yarn needle

Gauge in Pattern Stitch: 4 stitches = 1 inch; 4 rows = 1 inch (after blocking)

Strips: Make 2. With green, cast on 80 sts.
Row 1: *K 2, yo, k 4, sl 1, k 2 tog, psso, k 4, yo, rep from * across, ending k 2.
Row 2: P.
Rep Rows 1 and 2 for pat st, working in color sequence of (24 rows green, 12 rows rose) 6 times, ending with 24 rows green. Bind off.

Finishing: Sew the 2 strips tog with a running back st (see Stitch Glossary) on the wrong side of the work.

Tassels: Make 12 in rose, 13 in green. For each, cut eighteen 10-inch strands of yarn and tie a 7-inch strand around the middle. Fold the strands in half at the tie, wrap one end of one of the strands securely around the folded strands 1 inch below the tie, fasten off, and trim the ends evenly. Tie one tassel to each point on the two short edges, alternating the colors.

☞ **Handwork Hints:** This pattern stitch has a tendency to pull in, shrinking the width, so a careful blocking will be necessary. Use a damp cloth to block; then stretch the blanket out flat and weight each edge until it is dry.

12

Rattan

Approximate finished size: 53 by 57 inches

No Experience Needed

A simple, yet effective yarnover stitch creates the breezy look of this lightweight afghan. Since any number of striping patterns can be used with this stitch, you can follow your own whims.

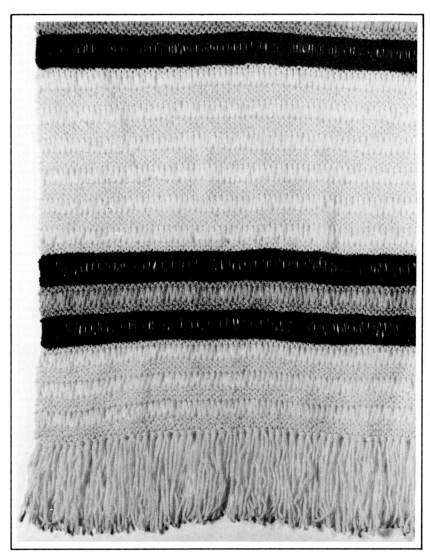

Materials:

Phildar Pegase, 50-gram (1¾-ounce) balls
    12 balls color 136, champagne (beige)
     1 ball color 104, horsechestnut (rust)
     1 ball color 174, flanelle (gray)
Knitting needles, No. 11
Yarn needle

Gauge in Pattern Stitch: 3 stitches = 1 inch

Strips: Make 3. With beige, cast on 53 sts.
Rows 1 through 4: K.
Row 5: K, wrapping yarn twice around working needle before drawing through each st.
Row 6: K, dropping off one extra yarnover with each st.
Rep Rows 1 through 6 twice more. Work Rows 1 and 2 once more. *Change to rust, work Rows 3 through 6, and then Rows 1 and 2. Change to gray, work Rows 3 through 6, and then Rows 1 and 2. Change to rust, work Rows 3 through 6, and then Rows 1 and 2. Change to beige, work Rows 3 through 6 once, Rows 1 through 6 five times, and then Rows 1 and 2. Rep from * twice more. Work rust-gray-rust stripe once more in same manner as established. Change to beige, work Rows 3 through 6 once, Rows 1 through 6 twice more, and end with Rows 1 through 4 once. Bind off.

Finishing: Sew strips tog with right side of work facing, working color over color and matching each row. Sew each garter-st (k every row) section separately with an overcast st (see Stitch Glossary), leaving the sts on the yarnover rows free.

Fringe: Cut 10-inch strands of beige yarn and knot 2 strands in every other st along top and bottom edges of afghan.

☞ **Handwork Hints:** If you have strong arms, you might like to eliminate the seams on this afghan by casting on 159 sts on long, circular needles (to hold all the yarnovers) and working it in one piece. Follow the striping pattern exactly as outlined in the instructions for the same length.

KNITTED LAP ROBES

13

Tiny Blossoms

Approximate finished size: 37 by 46 inches, including crocheted edging

No Experience Needed

Soft, white mohair squares are embroidered with clusters of pink French-knot blossoms with light green leaves. Each square is edged with a matching pink, single-crochet border. After the squares have been joined, a pink chain-loop border is crocheted all around. You might make a tiny pillow to match this delicate afghan, using one additional embroidered square with the pink crocheted edging worked for ten more rows. Back the pillow with a matching satin fabric and stuff. A lovely duet to adorn, perhaps, a velvet chaise lounge in a feminine bedroom.

Materials:
Mohair or wool/acrylic mohair-look yarn, 50-gram (1¾-ounce) balls (knitting worsted weight)
    6 balls white
    2 balls pink
    1 ball light green
Knitting needles, No. 10
Crochet hook, size F
Yarn needle

Gauge: 9 stitches = 2 inches; 5 rows = 1 inch

Squares: Make 20. With white, cast on 34 sts. Work even in St st (k 1 row, p 1 row) for 38 rows (7½ inches from beg). Bind off.

Finishing: Work 1 row of white, then 1 row of pink sc around each square, working 3 sc in each corner. Before joining, work embroidery on 10 of the 20 squares (see illustration A and "Handwork Hints"). Position the squares as shown in illustration B and join them with an overcast st (see Stitch Glossary) on the right side of work, sewing through the back lps of the pink sc sts with pink yarn.

Border: With pink, work around entire outside edge of blanket as follows:
Rnd 1: Join yarn in any sc, *1 sc in next st, ch 3, skip 1 st, rep from * around, join with sl st to first st.
Rnd 2: Sl st in each of first 2 ch, *ch 3, 1 sc in next ch-3 lp, rep from * around, join with sl st to first ch of rnd. Rep Rnd 2 twice more.

☞ **Handwork Hints:** The best method for transferring the embroidery design to the knitted squares is to copy the design in the center of a 7½-inch square of tracing paper. Pin the pattern to a knitted square and sew through the lines of the flower with a contrasting color of thread. Gently tear away the tracing paper and embroider along the thread guidelines you've now established. Experienced workers develop a reliable "eye" and a simple design such as this one can be worked free-hand.

Embroidery Design (A)

Color and Stitch Key:
Stem stitch in green ——
French knot in pink ●

Square Placement Diagram (B)

	X	X	
X			X
	X	X	
X			X
	X	X	

Key:
X *Embroidered square*

¹⁴ Arrowtip Lace

Approximate finished size: 41 by 49 inches

Worked in three strips on large needles, this overall "arrowtip lace" lap robe is made in pale rose and is finished with tassels along the top and bottom edges. This piece could be lined in a nonslip fabric, such as linen, in a contrasting color to give it an added dimension.

Materials:
Coats & Clark Red Heart 4-ply handknitting yarn, 3.5-ounce skeins (knitting worsted weight)
    6 skeins color 755, pale rose
Knitting needles, No. 11
Crochet hook, size G
Yarn needle

Gauge in Pattern Stitch: 3 stitches = 1 inch; 16 rows = 4 inches

Strips: Make 3. Cast on 41 sts.
Row 1 (right side): K 1, *yo, SKP, k 3, k 2 tog, yo, k 1, rep from * across.
Row 2 and all even rows: P.
Row 3: K 2, *yo, SKP, k 1, k 2 tog, yo, k 3, rep from * across, finishing last rep with k 2 instead of k 3.
Row 5: P 1, *k 2, yo, sl 1, k 2 tog, psso, yo, k 2, p 1, rep from * across.
Row 7: P 1, *SKP, k 1, (yo, k 1) twice, k 2 tog, p 1, rep from * across.
Rows 9, 11, 13, and 15: Work as for Row 7.
Row 16: P.
Rep Rows 1 through 16 eleven times more. Bind off.

Finishing: Sew strips tog on wrong side of work with an overcast st (see Stitch Glossary). Work 2 rows of sc around joined piece, working 3 sc in each corner.

Tassels: Make 62. For each tassel, cut five 10-inch strands of yarn and tie a 6-inch strand around the middle. Fold the strands in half at the tie, wrap one end of one of the strands securely around the folded strands 1 inch below the tie, fasten off, and trim the ends evenly. Tie 31 tassels evenly spaced along each of the two short edges.

☞ **Handwork Hints:** When working a fairly complicated pattern stitch such as this one, it's a good idea to make a practice swatch on the smallest number of multiples possible in order to familiarize yourself with the stitch. In this case, the multiple of the pattern stitch is 8 stitches plus 1, so cast on 9 stitches and work Rows 1 through 16 a few times. As you become more experienced, you'll begin to recognize the next stitch you need to make just by looking at the work in front of you. This little exercise will make a mistake on a larger number of stitches less likely. Also, if you want to avoid seaming strips together, you can cast on 121 stitches and work to the same length as the strips in the directions above.

Argyle Borders

Approximate finished size: 41 by 50 inches

Argyle breaks out of its traditional socks-and-sweater typecasting to border this gray lap robe with an understated lilac and yellow design. Those who are really ambitious can repeat the argyle design as many times as desired, even for the entire length of the blanket. An optional accent can be added by picking up the yellow diagonals only and extending them in duplicate stitch (see Stitch Glossary) for one or two more repeats of the pattern.

Materials:
Reynolds Reynelle, 4-ounce skeins (knitting worsted weight)
    6 skeins color 9054, medium gray
    2 skeins color 9053, lilac
    1 skein color 9011, yellow
Knitting needles, No. 10
Crochet hook, size H
Nine yarn bobbins
Yarn needle

Gauge: 4 stitches = 1 inch; 11 rows = 2 inches

Strips: Make 3. With gray, cast on 54 sts. Make hem: K 1 row, p 1 row, k 2 rows. Then work 52 rows of chart to completion, working in St st (k 1 row, p 1 row) throughout (see "Handwork Hints" for tips on how to work argyle pat). Work even in St st with gray only for 31 inches, ending on wrong side. Work chart in reverse (from Row 52 through Row 1). End p 2 rows, k 1 row, p 1 row. Bind off.

Finishing: Sew strips tog with running back st (see Stitch Glossary) on wrong side of work, carefully matching argyle pat. Fold hems to wrong side and tack in place. With gray, work 1 row of sc along each long edge followed by 1 row of reverse sc (work as for sc but work from left to right instead of right to left).

Fringe: Cut 11-inch lengths of yarn, 60 in lilac, 70 in yellow, and 360 in gray. Knot 5 strands of fringe in color and position as shown on chart.

☞ **Handwork Hints:** The use of bobbins has been advised so that the argyle pattern can be worked without strands of yarn having to be carried along the back. Wind 4 bobbins in yellow, 2 in lilac, and 3 in gray. The chart shows the stitch areas each bobbin will cover. Be sure to follow normal procedure when changing colors; that is, carry the old color to the left and bring the new color up from underneath to prevent gaps between colors.

Argyle Chart

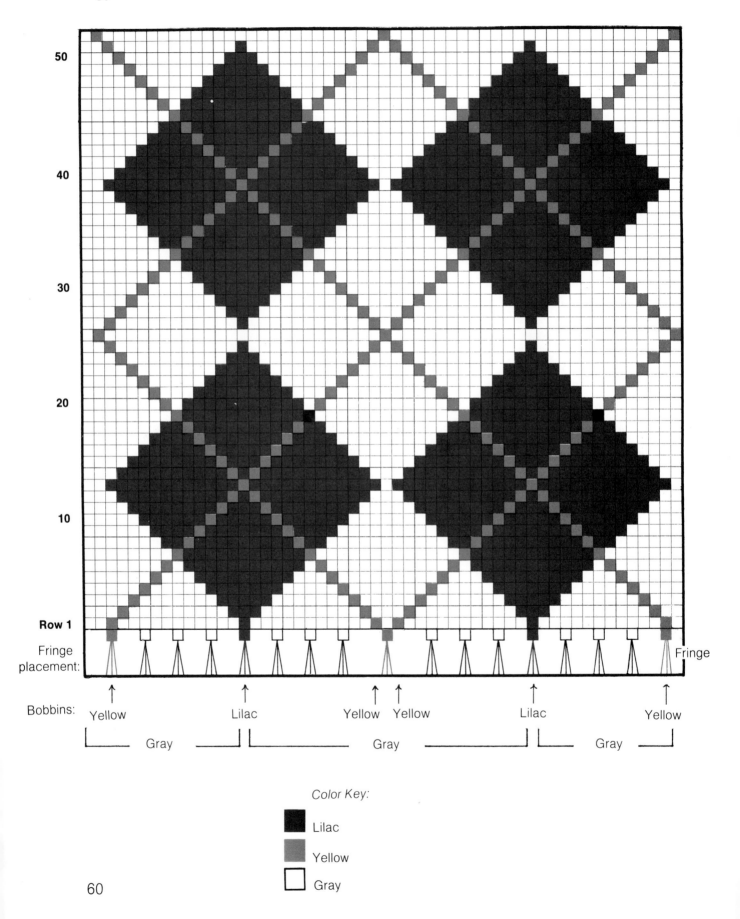

Color Key:

- ■ Lilac
- ▨ Yellow
- □ Gray

60

KNITTED BABY BLANKETS

16 Ribbons and Bows

Approximate finished size: 38 by 42 inches

No Experience Needed

This crib blanket is knitted in white stockinette stitch alternated with a simple pointelle stitch, thereby creating the spaces through which yards of pastel ribbons are beaded. Tiny bows in matching ribbon dot the blanket, making baby a pretty bundle indeed. Try using ribbon in just one bright color for a bolder effect or, for a more practical blanket for daily use, eliminate the ribbons and use multicolored crocheted chains instead.

Materials:
Knitting worsted, 4-ounce skeins
    5 skeins white
Knitting needles, No. 10½
Circular knitting needles, No. 10½
Ribbon, ⅜ inch wide:
    12 yards light green
     9 yards pink
     9 yards blue
Yarn needle

Gauge: 10 stitches = 3 inches

Note: Rows 3 and 4 of strip that follows will be referred to as reverse St st (p 1 row, k 1 row) under instructions for ribbon beading.

Strips: Make 3. Cast on 39 sts.
Row 1: K.
Row 2: P.
Row 3: P.
Row 4: K.
Rows 5 and 11: K 1, *yo, k 2 tog, rep from * across.
Rows 6 and 12: P.
Rows 7 and 9: K.
Rows 8 and 10: P.
Rep Rows 3 through 12 twenty times in all. End p 1 row, k 1 row, k 1 row, p 1 row. Bind off.

Finishing: Seam the 3 strips tog with an overcast st (see Stitch Glossary) on wrong side of work.

Border:
Row 1: With circular needles, pick up and k 1 st in the end of each row along one long edge of piece.
Row 2: P.
Row 3: K, inc 1 st in every other st across.
Row 4: P.
Row 5: Work as for Row 5 of strips.
Row 6: P.
Rep Rows 5 and 6 twice more. Bind off loosely. Rep on opposite edge of piece and then along each of the two short edges. Sew corners tog. Steam the border to block.

Ribbon Beading: First, frame the outside edge of the blanket with green ribbon by weaving as follows: *On long edges:* Weave over the 4 St-st rows and under the 2 rows of reverse St st. *On short edges:* Weave up from wrong side to right side through first yo sp, *skip 1 sp, weave down through next sp, up through the next sp, rep from * across, ending by weaving down through last sp. Sew the ends of the ribbons in place in the corners only. Now, following the diagram, weaving from top to bottom and from the center of diagram out, complete the diagonal beading of the ribbons through the yo sps, weaving over the 4 St-st rows and under the 2 reverse St-st rows.

☞ **Handwork Hints:** Circular needles are often used when a large number of stitches are to be knitted. Work back and forth in the usual manner for the border. When beading the ribbons, be sure that the piece is lying flat and straight, for this pattern stitch has a tendency to distort on the diagonal.

Ribbon Beading Chart

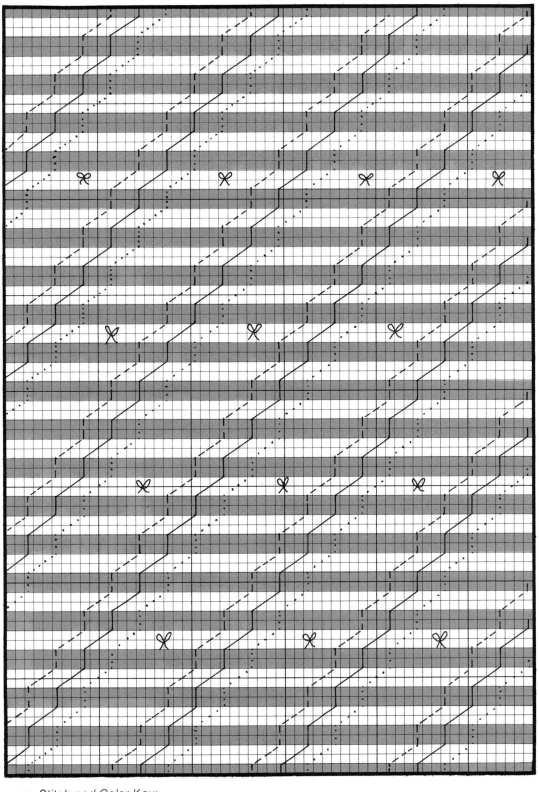

Stitch and Color Key:

☐ 4 rows stockinette stitch

▨ Adjacent rows of yarn-over spaces with 2 rows of reverse stockinette stitch between

- - - Light green ribbon

⸺ Blue ribbon

····· Pink ribbon

✣ Pink bow

Note: Each square along width of chart equals 1 yarn-over space. Also, when weaving under the 2 rows of reverse stockinette stitch, be sure to insert ribbon into the yarn-over space specified on chart and up through the space *directly* below it (see Chart).

17 Patchwork Hearts

Approximate finished size: 34 by 46 inches

Bright red, knit-in hearts on white squares alternate with white hearts on red squares to create this endearing afghan. To carry out its quilt style, doubled-over strips of red border the blanket all around. Look closely and you'll see that rather than each square having been worked separately, the square pattern has been knitted-in on five separate strips that have been joined. This design cuts finishing time considerably. Using the same design and techniques, you might extend the length and increase the number of strips to make a spectacular full-size bedspread for yourself.

Materials:
Sport yarn, 2-ounce balls
　　6 balls red
　　5 balls white
Knitting needles, No. 2
Yarn needle

Gauge: 13 stitches = 2 inches; 9 rows = 1 inch

Note: Work in St st (k 1 row, p 1 row) throughout.

Strip A: Make 3. With red, cast on 39 sts. *Using red as the background color and white for the heart, follow the 54-row chart to completion. Change to white for the background color and red for the heart and again work the chart to completion. Repeat from * 2 times more, and end with one more completion of the chart in the same colors as the first "square" of the strip—seven "squares" in all. Bind off.

Strip B: Make 2. With white, cast on 39 sts. Work in the same manner as for Strip A, but reverse the background and heart colors, beginning and ending with a white background square and alternating colors between (see photo).

Border: *Short strips:* Make 2. With red, cast on 25 sts. Work even for 32½ inches. Bind off. *Long strips:* Make 2. With red, cast on 25 sts. Work even for 44½ inches. Bind off.

Finishing: Referring to placement diagram for positioning, sew the heart strips tog on wrong side of work with a running back st (see Stitch Glossary). Referring again to placement diagram, position edges of border strips along edges of main piece right side against right side. Using red thread, join with a running back st. Now turn each strip to right side, fold in half, and overcast (see Stitch Glossary) free edge to wrong-side edge of main piece. Turn short edges of strips inward and sew them tog where they meet or where they extend to outside edge; gently block the piece.

☞ **Handwork Hints:** When sewing the strips together, be careful to match opposing color row to opposing color row exactly, for the beauty of the design is in its sharp positive-negative contrast. For an extra-fine finishing job, join the border strips so that the short end of one strip can be inserted into the extended open end of another strip where they meet in the corners; studying the photo before beginning may be helpful in visualizing this.

Heart Stitch Chart

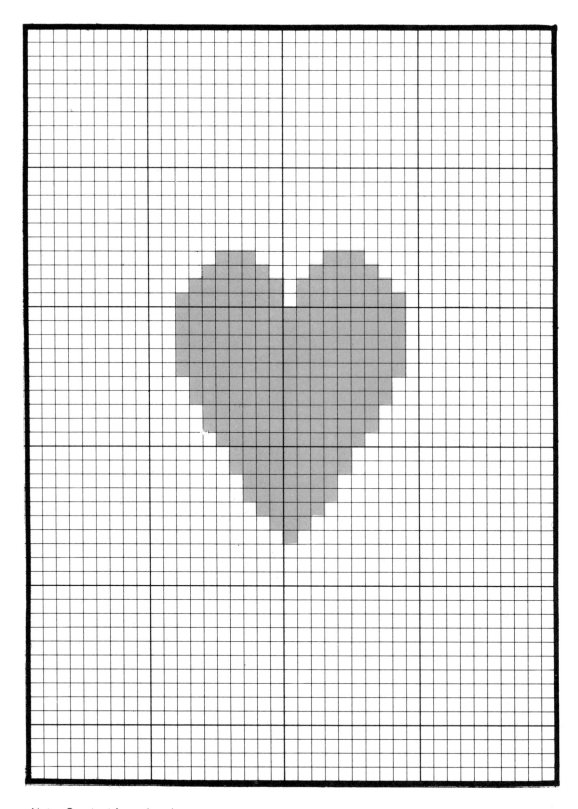

Note: See text for color changes.

Placement Diagram

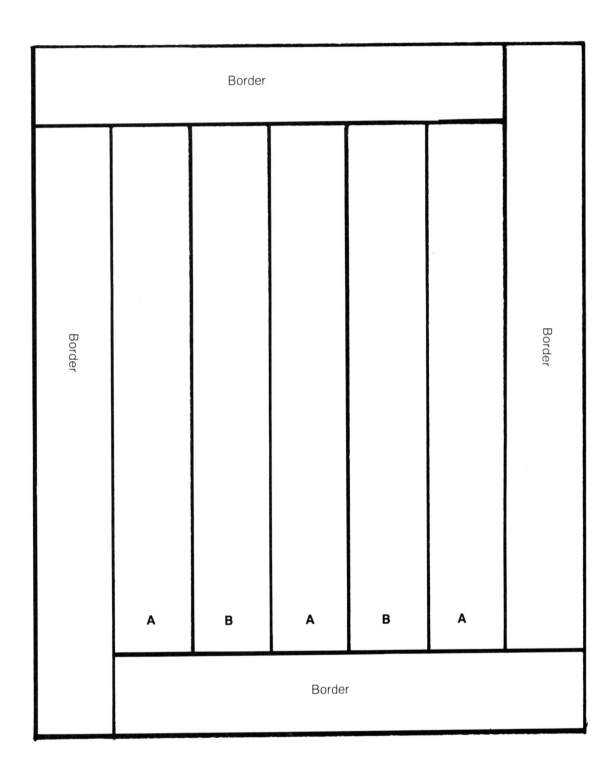

⒅ Baby Smocking

Approximate finished size: 30 by 33 inches

No Experience Needed

A very simple, blue ribbed background is worked over with a rose smocking stitch to warm any baby boy or girl. This carriage-size blanket is so simple to make that you will have no difficulty enlarging it to crib, lap-robe, or even afghan size.

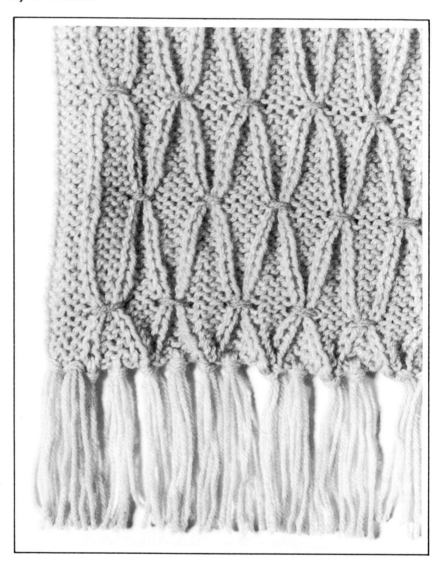

Materials:
Phildar Leader, 100-gram (3.5-ounce) balls (knitting worsted weight)
    5 balls color 23, pastel blue
    1 ball color 05, empire rose
Knitting needles, No. 8
Yarn needle

Gauge in Pattern Stitch: 4 stitches = 1 inch; 9 rows = 2 inches

Note: We worked this blanket in one piece because the number of stitches needed for a carriage-size blanket is not large.

Pattern Stitch:
Row 1: P 3, *k 1, p 3, rep from * across.
Row 2: K 3, *p 1, k 3, rep from * across.
Rep Rows 1 and 2 for pat st.

Background: Make 1. With blue, cast on 155 sts and work in pat st for 150 rows. Bind off.

Finishing: Turn the first and last 3 p sts on long edges of piece to wrong side of work and sew in place with an overcast st (see Stitch Glossary).

Smocking: Thread the yarn needle with rose and, starting at the lower right-hand corner and working to the left, work as follows:
Row 1: *Insert needle from back to front of work after the third k st of the fifth row (count the st on the very right-hand edge of the blanket as the first k st), *bring the yarn back to the right across the front of the k st, the next 3 p sts, and the next k st, insert needle from front to back after this k st, draw yarn through, and work once more in same manner over the embroidered st just made. Skip the next (p 3, k 1) twice, insert needle from back to front of the work after the last k st, rep from * across, ending by embroidering the second and third k sts from the left edge tog as established, leaving the last (p 3, k 1) free to correspond to beg of row at right-hand edge.
Row 2: Go back to right edge of work, skip the first 4 k sts on the tenth row above last smocked row, work the smocking st over the third and fourth k sts of the row as established on the previous row and continue across, leaving the last 2 k sts of the row free to correspond to beg of row. Fasten off.
Row 3: Go back to right edge of work. Skip the first 3 k sts on the tenth row above last smocked row and work smocking across, lining up the sts with the first row of smocking.
Rep Rows 2 and 3 to complete the smocking, ending with a

Row 3 and leaving the last 5 rows free to correspond to the first 5 rows at the bottom of the blanket. Lightly block the hem at each side edge of the blanket.

Fringe: Cut 8-inch strands of blue yarn and knot 6 strands in each st as follows: Working from right to left, knot 1 set of fringe in k st at edge, 1 set in second p st of next p-3, 1 set in next k st, *1 set in second p st of next p-3, insert hook from back to front through each of next 2 k sts, bringing the 2 sts tog to form a point, and knot 1 set through these 2 k sts, rep from * across, ending row to correspond to beg of row. Trim the ends evenly.

☞ **Handwork Hints:** Long threads will have been carried across the back of the blanket when the embroidery is finished. A lining can be sewn to the back of the blanket to cover these threads. Satin in a matching blue would be pretty, but a nonslip material, such as linen, would be more practical.

CROCHETED AFGHANS

19

Neon Granny

Approximate finished size: 43 by 68 inches, including French fringe

Granny squares in shocking pink, turquoise, and yellow get a facelift with this fresh treatment of an old form. Grannies are joined in three V-shaped groups, from which point each of the groups is worked on in black and multicolor stripes and then joined to create an electric effect.

Materials:
Phildar Pronostic, 50-gram (1¾-ounce) balls (sport yarn)
    5 balls color 67, noir (black)
    5 balls color 89, soleil (yellow)
    3 balls color 94, turquoise
    3 balls color 37, fuchsia (pink)
Crochet hook, size G
Yarn needle

Gauge: 3 double crochet = 1 inch; each square = 5 inches

Granny Squares: Make 10 in pink, 10 in turquoise, 8 in yellow. Ch 6, join with sl st to form a ring.
Rnd 1: Ch 2, 2 dc in ring, (ch 1, 3 dc in ring) 3 times, ch 1, join with sl st to second ch of starting ch-2. Sl st across next 2 dc to first ch-1 sp.
Rnd 2: Sl st in first ch-1 sp, ch 2, (2 dc, ch 1, 3 dc) in same ch-1 sp, *(3 dc, ch 1, 3 dc) in next ch-1 sp—corner made, rep from * twice more. Join with sl st to second ch of starting ch-2. Sl st across next 2 dc to first ch-1 sp.
Rnd 3: Sl st in first ch-1 sp, ch 2, (2 dc, ch 1, 3 dc) in same ch-1 sp, *3 dc between next two 3-dc groups, work corner (see Rnd 2) in next ch-1 sp, rep from * twice more, ending 3 dc between next two 3-dc groups. Join with sl st to second ch of starting ch-2. Sl st across next 2 dc to first ch-1 sp.
Rnds 4 and 5: Work as for Rnd 3, adding one more repeat of (3 dc between next two 3-dc groups) between corners on each successive row. Fasten off.

V-Stripes: Sew granny squares tog with an overcast st (see Stitch Glossary) in three separate groups as shown in placement diagram, leaving the single pink square in the lower left-hand corner unattached.

Striping Pattern: Working along two sides only of the unattached pink square through back lps only, proceed as follows: *Row 1:* Attach turquoise in ch-1 st of any corner sp, work 1 sc in each st along first side of square, work 3 sc in next corner ch-1 st, continue in sc along next side only, ending with 1 sc in ch-1 st of next corner. Fasten off. Return to beg of row.
Row 2: Attach black in first st of previous row, ch 2, work 1 dc in each st along first side to center corner st, 3 dc in center st, continue in dc along next side only. Fasten off. Return to beg of row.
Row 3: Work as for Row 2, but work in yellow sc.
Rep Rows 2 and 3 six times more, working each Row 2 in black dc and alternating the following colors on each of the consecutive Row-3 repeats in this order: (pink, turquoise, yellow) twice. Work along the two outside edges of each of the three joined granny-square groups in the same manner

(work along each of the squares to the corner st of corner granny square, 3 sts in corner st, and proceed along each of the remaining squares). (See placement diagram.)

Finishing: Sew the four V-shaped groups tog with yellow and overcast st (see Stitch Glossary), as shown in placement diagram. Work 1 row of black sc along the short, unstriped edge of the joined piece. Now work the 15-row stripe pat along this edge only.

Border: Work 3 rows of yellow sc around entire piece, working through both lps of all sc sts and working 2 sc into the dc sts on outside edge with 3 sc in each corner. Fasten off.

French Fringe: Cut 18-inch strands of yellow yarn and knot 5 strands in every fourth st along the two short edges of afghan. Then *knot 5 strands of first group of fringe to 5 strands of the next group 1½ inches below the original knot; rep from * across. In same manner, work 1 more row of knots 1½ inches below the last row. Trim the ends evenly. Rep on remaining short edge.

☞ **Handwork Hints:** Rather than working this afghan in four separate sections, you can sew the granny squares together in the groups as shown and then work the first stripe pattern around the unattached pink square, sew the next group of grannies to the first completed stripe section around the pink square, and work the stripe pattern around the group just joined, working in the same manner with each consecutive group. After the last stripe has been worked, the entire afghan will already have been joined and you can proceed to work the border as outlined above.

Placement Diagram

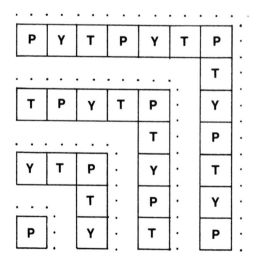

Color Key:
P Pink
T Turquoise
Y Yellow
... edge along which 15-row stripe is worked

20

Victorian Openwork

Approximate finished size: 48 by 60 inches

Worked in cream color, two narrow strips of simple open-mesh filet and three wide strips of the same filet with a vine pattern are joined for an old-fashioned effect minus the old-fashioned effort, as they are worked with a relatively large hook and medium-weight crochet cotton. The vine-patterned strips could also be used as inserts on a folding-screen room divider, hung with crocheted tabs from a rod from the ceiling, or stretched between top and bottom rods on a glass door.

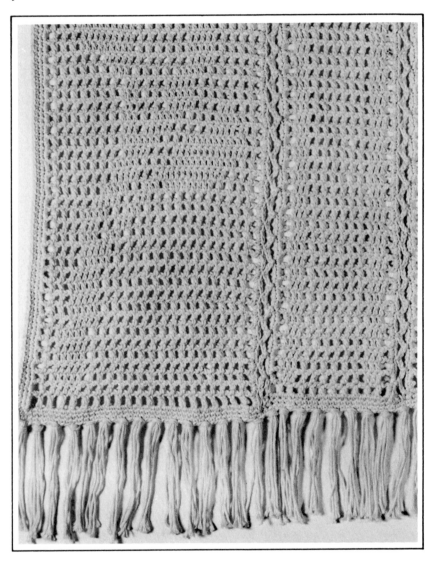

Materials:
Coats & Clark Red Heart 100% Cotton Knit & Crochet Yarn, 2.5-ounce skeins (medium-weight crochet cotton)
    16 skeins color 108, cream
Crochet hook, size F

Gauge: (1 dc, ch 1, 1 dc, ch 1, 1 dc) = 1 inch; 2 rows = 1 inch

Note: To read chart, count each vertical line of graph grids as 1 dc to be worked in the dc of row below, each dotted square as 1 dc to be worked in the ch-1 sp of row below, and each blank square as a ch-1 sp. Always ch 4 to turn (counts as first dc and ch-1 sp of next row) and work last dc of each row in third ch of turning ch-4 of previous row.

Vine-Pattern Strips: Make 3. Ch 46.
Row 1: Starting in sixth ch from hook, work 1 dc, *ch 1, skip 1 ch, dc in next ch, rep from * across (twenty-one ch-1 sps). Now work vine chart to completion, starting with Row 2.

Narrow Strips: Make 2. Ch 26.
Row 1: Starting in sixth ch from hook, work 1 dc, *ch 1, skip 1 ch, 1 dc in next ch, rep from * across (11 ch-1 sps). Ch 4, turn.
Row 2: Skip first dc and ch-1 sp, 1 dc in next dc, 1 dc in next ch-1 sp, 1 dc in next dc, (ch 1, 1 dc in next dc) 7 times, 1 dc in next ch-1 sp, 1 dc in next dc, ch 1, 1 dc in third ch of turning ch-4 of previous row. Ch 4, turn.
Row 3: Skip first dc and ch-1 sp, 1 dc in each of next 3 dc, (ch 1, 1 dc in next dc) 7 times, 1 dc in each of next 2 dc, ch 1, 1 dc in third ch of turning ch-4 of previous row. Ch 4, turn. Rep Row 3 for a total of 119 rows from beg. *Last Row:* Work in filet-mesh pat for 11 ch-1 sps.

Finishing: Work 1 row of sc around each strip, working 2 sc around the dc at end of each row and 5 sc in each corner.

Zigzag Joining: Position the strips so that one vine strip is on each outside edge with the remaining vine strip and two narrow strips alternated between. Starting at the right-hand bottom edge of afghan and working toward the top, join yarn at bottom right-hand corner st of first narrow strip (to be called left strip from now on), ch 3, remove hook and insert in bottom left-hand corner st of vine strip (to be called right strip from now on), pick up dropped ch-lp, draw through, yo, draw through, ch 3, remove hook, skip 2 sc on left strip edge, *insert hook in next st, pick up dropped ch-lp, draw through, yo, draw through, ch 3, remove hook, skip 3 sc on right strip edge, insert hook in next st, pick up dropped ch-lp, draw through, yo, draw through, ch 3, remove hook, skip 3 sc on left strip edge, rep from * until the two strips are completely joined, ending by working ch-3 between the two corner sts of each strip, join with sl st, and fasten off. Work this same joining 3 times more between the remaining strips. Now, work 2 rnds of sc around entire joined piece, working 3 sc in each corner.

Fringe: Cut 10-inch lengths of string and knot 4 strands in every third st along top and bottom edges of afghan.

☞ **Handwork Hints:** When making any blanket with more than one strip design, always double-check to make sure that you have the same number of rows on each strip, in this case 120 rows, so that the joining will be perfect. Also, after you have finished your first Vine-Pattern Strip, you may find it easier to follow your completed strip for the remaining two pieces rather than the chart.

Vine Pattern Strip Chart
(see text for key)

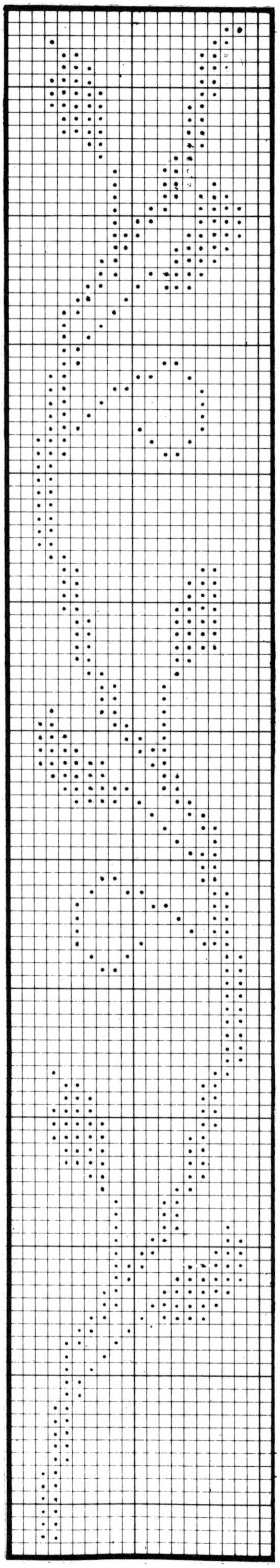

Clockwise from bottom: *Crayon Stripes, p. 119; Parrot, p. 106; Flowers at the Crossroads, p. 96.*

Clockwise from bottom: *Snowflakes, p. 44; Icelandic Accent, p. 39; Portable Lap Robe, p. 126.*

From left to right: *Victorian Openwork, p. 77; Berry Stitch Get-Together, p. 93; Chevron Stripes, p. 49.*

Clockwise from bottom: *Lightning Strikes, p. 102; Squares in the Round, p. 35; Neon Granny, p. 74.*

From left to right: *Navajo Symbols, p. 122; Patchwork Hearts, p. 66; Blue Willow, p. 116.*

Clockwise from bottom: *Harlequin, p. 47; Stitch Sampler, p. 129; All Points, p. 29.*

From left to right: *Baby's Bouquet, p. 141; Fiesta, p. 134; Pandas on Parade, p. 137.*

From left to right: *Irish Knit Updated, p. 31; Arrowtip Lace, p. 56; Log Cabin Quilt, p. 26.*

From left to right: *Argyle Borders, p. 58; Grapevines (floor), p. 99; Fan and Feather, p. 37; Woven Pastel Plaid, p. 89.*

Above: *Motifs Ahoy, p. 110.* Left: *Rattan, p. 51.* Right: *Seascape, p. 20.*

From left to right: *Ribbons and Bows, p. 62; Tiny Blossoms, p. 54; Baby Smocking, p. 70.*

From left to right: *Flowing Lace, p. 42; Colonial Ripples, p. 114.*

21

Woven Pastel Plaid

Approximate finished size: 50 by 62 inches

No Experience Needed

Three strips of misty lavender mohair, each made partly in solid double crochet and partly in open mesh work, are woven across, horizontally and vertically, with crocheted chains of lightest green and off-white. Extravagant, 6-inch-long fringe in color-over-color pattern trims the edges. A beginner will be proud of the effect that this blanket of basic stitches creates. Be sure to read "Handwork Hints" before beginning the weaving and edging.

Materials:
Pingouin Laine et Mohair, 50-gram (1¾-ounce) balls
(medium-weight mohair)

     13 balls color 52, glycine (purple)

      4 balls color 28, vert d'eau (light green)

      3 balls color 40, ecru (off-white)

Crochet hook, size J
Yarn needle

Gauge (before weaving): 3 double crochet = 1 inch; 3 rows = 2 inches

Strips: Make 3. With purple, ch 51.
Row 1: Starting in fourth ch from hook, work 1 dc in each of next 6 ch, (ch 1, skip 1 ch, 1 dc in next ch) 3 times, 1 dc in each of next 24 ch, (ch 1, skip 1 ch, 1 dc in next ch) 3 times, 1 dc in each of next 6 ch. Ch 2 (counts as first dc of next row), turn.
Rows 2 through 6: Maintain pat st as established on Row 1. Ch 2 to turn at end of each row.
Rows 7 through 11: *Ch 1, skip next st, 1 dc in next st, rep from * across row (24 ch-1 sps).
Rows 12 through 25: Work as for Row 2.
Rows 26 through 30: Work as for Rows 7 through 11.
Rep Rows 12 through 30 three times more and then work Rows 12 through 17 once more. Fasten off.

Finishing: Overcast (see Stitch Glossary) strips tog on wrong side of work, sewing last dc on edge of one strip to first dc on edge of next strip, matching rows as you go.

Chains: *Long chains:* Make 12 in light green and 6 in off-white. Using double strands of yarn, crochet a chain long enough to weave along length of afghan—approximately 62 inches. Fasten off. *Short chains:* Make 15 in light green and 10 in off-white. Using double strands of yarn, make a chain long enough to weave along width of afghan—approximately 52 inches. Fasten off by hand.

Horizontal Weaving (along width): Starting in lower right-hand corner of blanket with a short light-green chain, bring chain up from wrong side to right side through first sp of Row 7 and then weave as follows: Over next 2 sps, under next dc, *over next 3 sps, under next dc, rep from * across width of blanket to last 3 sps, weave over next 2 sps and down through last sp. Rep in same manner along Rows 8 through 11, using off-white chains on Rows 8 and 10 and light green on Rows 9 and 11. Complete remaining four horizontal mesh sections in same manner.

Vertical Weaving (along length): Starting in lower right-hand corner of blanket with a long light-green chain, bring chain up from wrong side to right side through first sp of Row 1 and then weave as follows: Over next 2 sps, under next ch-1, over next 3 sps, under next ch-1, *over next 5 horizontal woven chains (5 sps), under next ch-1, over next 4 sps, under next ch-1, (over next 3 sps, under next ch-1) twice, over next 4 sps, under next ch-1, rep from * 3 times more, ending by weaving over last 5 horizontal woven chains, under next ch-1, over next 3 sps, under next ch-1, over next 2 sps, down through last sp. Rep in same manner along next 2 vertical rows of sps, using off-white on next row and light green on next. Complete remaining 5 vertical mesh sections in same manner.

Single-Crochet Edging: With purple and working loosely, work 1 row of sc around entire blanket, working 3 sc in each corner, 1 sc in each dc or ch-1 sp along top and bottom edges, and 1 sc around each dc along the two side edges of the blanket. At the same time, when working around or in a dc or ch-1 sp at the end of a woven chain, insert hook around the dc, through the woven chain, pull up a lp through the chain, and complete the sc st, thereby securing the end of the chain.

Fringe: Cut 12-inch lengths of purple yarn and knot 3 strands in every other sc along edge of blanket except along the ends of the woven chains. Cut 12-inch lengths of off-white and light green and knot 3 strands in the sc st, color over color, at end of each chain (see photo). Trim ends evenly.

☞ **Handwork Hints:** Don't worry, as you are working, about the mesh sections of the strips being narrower than the solid double-crochet sections, for the weaving will even things out. Before starting the weaving, stretch the joined piece out as flat as possible, on the floor perhaps, and complete the weaving in this position to achieve an even tension. To save yourself some trouble later, weave the chains so that the beginning (first stitch) of each chain is positioned along the same long edge of afghan and the next short edge to the left of it. The reason for this will be explained later. When working the single-crochet edging around, first work along the long and short edges where the first stitch of each chain was placed. Lay the piece flat once again and stretch the chains out. You can now unravel each chain, if necessary, to the exact length needed and fasten off. It was for this reason that you placed the beginning stitch of each horizontal and vertical chain along the same edges of the afghan. Now you can complete the rest of the edging with the knowledge that your woven chains are exactly the right length. Also, when knotting the fringe in the color-over-color sections (see instructions), try to knot the fringe into the end of the woven chain so that the purple single crochet on the edge of the afghan is covered and the chain color extends smoothly from the chain into the fringe.

22 Berry Stitch Get-Together

Approximate finished size: 49 by 61 inches

Experienced Crocheters Only

Raspberry-pink squares of double crochet with berry stitches strategically placed in each corner create an unexpected design at the intersections when joined together. The squares were worked on a tight gauge, but you can loosen it up by using a larger hook if desired. The antique look of this afghan could be heightened even more if it were made in an ecru or antique beige yarn. Experienced crocheters should expect a good challenge from this one. It is time-consuming but well worth the effort to create a treasure that will be passed on proudly from generation to generation.

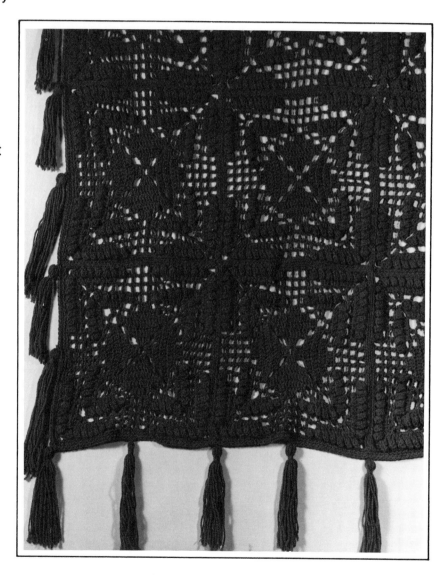

Materials:
Reynolds Reynelle, 100-gram (3.5-ounce) balls (knitting worsted weight)
    12 balls color 9026, raspberry
Crochet hook, size F
Yarn needle

Gauge: 4 double crochet = 1 inch; each square = approximately 12 inches

Note: To make berry stitch, work 5 dc in same sp or st, remove hook, insert hook in first dc, pull dropped lp through first dc.

Squares: Make 20. Ch 8, join with sl st to form a ring.
Rnd 1: Ch 3, 3 dc in ring, ch 5, (4 dc in ring, ch 5) 3 times. Join with sl st to third ch of starting ch-3.
Rnd 2: Ch 3, work 1 dc in each of next 3 dc, work *2 dc in next ch-5 lp, (dc, ch 5, dc) in third ch of same ch-5 lp— corner made, 2 dc in same ch-5 lp, 1 dc in each of next 4 dc, rep from * twice more, end 2 dc in last ch-5 lp, corner (see above), 2 dc in same ch-5 lp. Join with sl st to third ch of starting ch-3.
Rnd 3: Ch 3, work 1 dc in each of next 6 dc, *2 dc in next ch-5 lp, corner (see Rnd 2), 2 dc in same ch-5 lp, 1 dc in each of next 10 dc, rep from * twice more, end 2 dc in last ch-5 lp, corner, 2 dc in same ch-5 lp, 1 dc in each of next 3 dc. Join with sl st to third ch of starting ch-3.
Rnd 4: Ch 3, 1 dc in each of next 6 dc, *ch 2, skip 2 dc, 1 dc in next dc, ch 2, corner, ch 2, 1 dc in next dc, ch 2, skip 2 dc, 1 dc in each of next 10 dc, rep from * twice more, end ch 2, skip 2 dc, 1 dc in next dc, ch 2, corner, ch 2, 1 dc in next dc, ch 2, skip 2 dc, 1 dc in each of next 3 dc. Join with sl st to third ch of starting ch-3.
Rnd 5: Ch 3, 1 dc in each of next 3 dc, *ch 2, skip 2 dc, 1 dc in next dc, ch 2, 1 dc in next dc, 2 dc in next ch-2 sp, 1 dc in next dc, 2 dc in next ch-5 sp, corner, 2 dc in same ch-5 sp, 1 dc in next dc, 2 dc in next ch-2 sp, 1 dc in next dc, ch 2, 1 dc in next dc, ch 2, skip 2 dc, 1 dc in each of next 4 dc, rep from * twice more, end ch 2, skip 2 dc, 1 dc in next dc, ch 2, 1 dc in next dc, 2 dc in next ch-2 sp, 1 dc in next dc, 2 dc in next ch-5 sp, corner, 2 dc in same ch-5 sp, 1 dc in next dc, 2 dc in next ch-2 sp, 1 dc in next dc, ch 2, 1 dc in next dc, ch 2. Join with sl st to third ch of starting ch-3.
Rnd 6: Ch 5, skip 2 dc, 1 dc in next dc, ch 2, 1 dc in next dc, *1 berry in next ch-2 sp, 1 dc in same sp, (1 berry in next dc, 1 dc in next dc) 3 times, 1 berry in next dc, corner, (1 berry in next dc, 1 dc in next dc) 3 times, 1 berry in next dc, 1 dc in next ch-2 sp, 1 berry in same ch-2 sp, 1 dc in next dc, ch 2 **, 1 dc in next dc, ch 2, skip 2 dc, 1 dc in next dc, ch 2, 1 dc in next dc, rep from * twice more, then from * to ** once. Join

with sl st to third ch of starting ch-5.

Rnd 7: Ch 5, 1 dc in next dc, ch 2, 1 dc in next dc, *ch 2, skip 2 berries, 1 dc in next dc, (ch 2, dc in next dc) 3 times, ch 2, corner, (ch 2, 1 dc in next dc) 4 times, ch 2, skip 2 berries, 1 dc in next dc, (ch 2**, 1 dc in next dc) 3 times, rep from * twice more, then from * to ** once. Join with sl st to third ch of starting ch-5.

Rnd 8: Ch 5, 1 dc in next dc, (ch 2, 1 dc in next dc) 3 times, *(2 dc in next ch-2 sp, 1 dc in next dc) 3 times, corner, (1 dc in next dc, 2 dc in next ch-2 sp) 3 times, 1 dc in next dc **, (ch 2, 1 dc in next dc) 7 times, rep from * twice more, then from * to ** once, end (ch 2, 1 dc in next dc) twice, ch 2, join with sl st to third ch of starting ch-5.

Rnd 9: Ch 5, 1 dc in next dc, (ch 2, 1 dc in next dc) twice, *1 berry in next ch-2 sp, 1 dc in same ch-2 sp, (1 berry in next dc, 1 dc in next dc) 5 times, 1 berry in next dc, corner, (1 berry in next dc, 1 dc in next dc) 5 times, 1 berry in next dc, 1 dc in next ch-2 sp, 1 berry in same sp, 1 dc in next dc**, (ch 2, 1 dc in next dc) 5 times, rep from * twice more, then from * to ** once, ch 2, 1 dc in next dc, ch 2. Join with sl st to third ch of starting ch-5.

Finishing: Work 1 row of sc around each square, working 7 sc in each ch-5 corner lp. Sew squares tog, four squares wide by five squares long, with overcast st (see Stitch Glossary) on wrong side of work. Work 2 rows of sc around joined piece. Block the joined piece.

Tassels: Make 36. Cut thirteen 12-inch strands of yarn and tie a 7-inch strand around the middle. Fold the strands in half at the tie, wrap one end of one of the strands securely around the folded strands 1 inch below the tie, fasten off, and trim the ends evenly. Tie one tassel in each corner of the afghan at the end of each seam and in the center of the edge of each square.

☞ **Handwork Hints:** When each square is completed, it will have a ruffled appearance that needs to be blocked out, but this need not be done before joining. After the piece has been joined, block with a wet towel on the wrong side of the work, pulling each square out to make the edges straight. Allow the piece to dry flat. After the piece is dry, fluff up the berries, which may have been flattened during the blocking.

₂₃ Flowers at the Crossroads

Approximate finished size: 48 by 58 inches from point to point

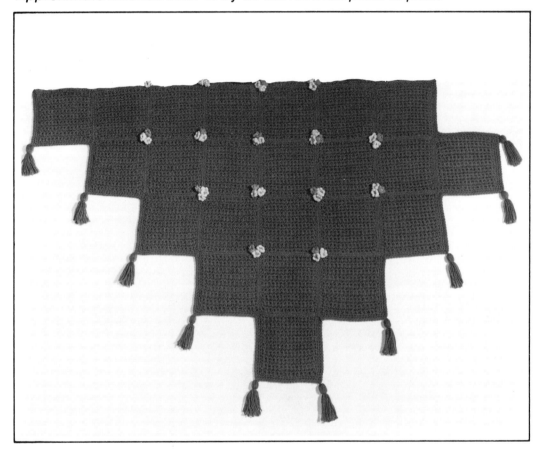

Grass-green plots of textured crochet are met at each intersection by a trio of flowers in goldenrod, orange blossom, and vermilion. Each bouquet is crocheted separately and then appliquéd to the main piece. A thick bundle of green yarn makes the tassel at each outer point to finish a country-fresh afghan that will brighten any room.

Materials:
Pingouin Pingochamp, 100-gram (3.5-ounce) skeins (knitting worsted weight)
  11 skeins color 358, bright green
  1 skein color 302, goldenrod
  1 skein color 306, orange blossom
  1 skein color 308, vermilion
Crochet hooks, sizes G and I
Yarn needle

Gauge: 2 pattern stitches = 1 inch; 2 rows = 1 inch

Squares: Make 32. With green and size I hook, ch 27.
Row 1: Insert hook in third ch from hook, *yo, draw through, skip 1 ch, insert hook in next ch, yo, draw through, (yo, draw through 2 lps on hook) twice, ch 1, insert hook in same ch as last st, rep from * across, ending skip 1 ch, insert hook in last ch, yo, draw through, (yo, draw through 2 lps on hook) twice, sc in same ch as last st. Ch 2, turn.
Row 2: Insert hook in last sc of previous row, yo, draw through, *insert hook in next ch-1 sp, yo, draw through, (yo, draw through 2 lps on hook) twice, ch 1, insert hook in same ch-1 sp as last st, yo, draw through, rep from * across, ending insert hook in second ch of turning ch-2, yo, draw through, (yo, draw through 2 lps on hook) twice, 1 sc in same ch. Ch 2, turn. Rep Row 2 until there are 17 rows in all. Fasten off.

Edging: With green, work 1 row of sc around each square, working the same number of sts on each side of square and 3 sc in each corner. Sew the squares tog as shown on the placement diagram. Work 2 rows of sc around the entire joined piece, working 3 sc in each of the outer points and skipping 2 sts at each of the indentations.

Flowers: Make 17 in each of goldenrod, orange blossom, and vermilion. With size G hook, ch 2.
Rnd 1: Work 5 sc in second ch from hook, join with sl st to first st.
Rnd 2: Work 1 sc in first sc, ch 3, sl st in same sc, work (sc, ch 3, sc) in each of the remaining 4 sc, join with sl st to first st. Fasten off.
Group together one of each of the three colors of flowers, place each group on the afghan as shown on the diagram, and attach each flower through its center with a French knot, using goldenrod yarn for the vermilion flowers and vermilion for the others (see photo).

Tassels: Make 18. For each, cut twenty 10-inch strands of green yarn and tie around the center with a 7-inch strand. Fold the strands in half at the tie, wrap one end of one of the strands around the yarn 1 inch below the tie, fasten off, and

Placement Diagram

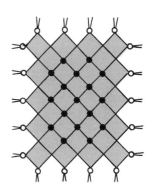

Key:

● Three-flower group

Ω Tassel

◆ Crocheted square

trim the ends evenly. Tie one tassel at each of the outer points of the afghan, as shown on the diagram.

☞ **Handwork Hints:** When sewing the squares together on this afghan, or on any piece with a single-crochet edging, you can make a beautiful seam by working on the wrong side of the work with an overcast stitch (see Stitch Glossary) that picks up just the horizontal thread on the back of each single crochet. This technique leaves the two loops on the top of the single-crochet edging intact for a well-delineated seam on the right side of the work.

²⁴ Grapevines

Approximate finished size: 47 by 53 inches

Deep purple grapes growing on neon-green vines climb vertically on a black, textured background strip contrasted with crocheted-lace strips. The grapes are crocheted in, while the vines are crocheted separately and appliquéd after the strips have been completed and joined. Other possible background colors could be off-white or light lavender. Those experienced with embroidery might prefer to embroider the vines and leaves, using chain stitch and satin stitch respectively (see Stitch Glossary).

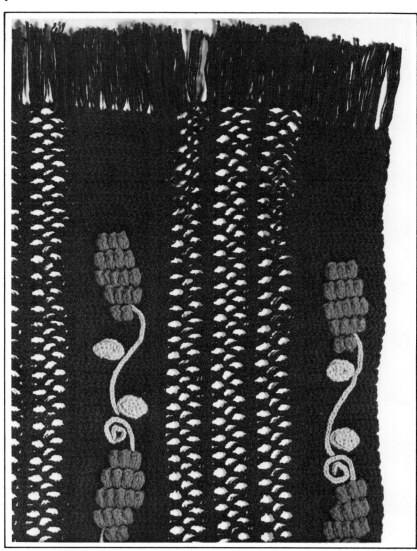

Materials:
Coats & Clark Red Heart Preference, 100-gram (3.5-ounce) skeins

      10 skeins color 12, black
       1 skein color 588, amethyst
       1 skein color 281, green apple

Crochet hooks, sizes J and H
Yarn needle

Gauge: 3 stitches = 1 inch; 5 rows (1 row sc, 1 row dc) twice, 1 row sc = 2 inches

Note: To make one grape, work 5 dc in 1 st, remove hook, insert hook in first dc, pull dropped lp through first dc.

Grapevine Strips: Make 4. With black and J hook, ch 16.
Background Stitch:
Row 1 (wrong side): Work 1 sc in second ch from hook and each ch across (15 sts). Ch 2, turn.
Row 2: Work 1 dc in each sc across. Ch 1, turn.
Row 3: Work 1 sc in each dc across. Ch 2, turn.
Rep Rows 2 and 3 for pat st until there are 17 rows in all (end with wrong-side row).
Grape Bunch:
Row 1 (right side): With black, work 1 dc in each of first 7 sc, taking last 2 lps of last dc off with purple. Work 1 purple grape (see Note) in each of next 2 sc, pulling black through dropped lp and first dc of last grape. With black, work 1 dc in each of remaining 6 sc. Ch 1, turn.
Rows 2, 4, 6, 8, and 10: With black, work across in sc, being sure to maintain 15 sts. Ch 2, turn.
Row 3: With black and changing colors when necessary as outlined on Row 1, work 1 dc in each of first 6 sc, 1 purple grape in each of next 4 sc, 1 dc in each of remaining 5 sc. Ch 1, turn.
Row 5: With black, work 1 dc in each of first 5 sc, 1 grape in each of next 5 sc, 1 dc in each of remaining 5 sc. Ch 1, turn.
Row 7: With black, work 1 dc in each of first 5 sc, 1 grape in each of next 4 sc, 1 dc in each of remaining 6 sc. Ch 1, turn.
Row 9: Work 1 dc in each of first 5 sc, 1 grape in each of next 3 sc, 1 dc in each of next 7 sc.
Rep Rows 2 and 3 of background st 8 times in all (16 rows). Work the 10 rows of the grape bunch followed by 16 rows in background stitch 3 times more. Fasten off.

Lace Strips: Make 3. With J hook and black, ch 30 loosely.
Row 1: Work 1 sc in each of second and third chs from hook, *ch 5, skip 3 ch, 1 sc in next ch, ch 5, skip 3 ch, 1 sc in each of next 2 ch, rep from * across. Ch 3, turn.
Row 2: Work 1 dc in second sc, *ch 2, 1 sc in next ch-5 lp, ch 5, 1 sc in next ch-5 lp, ch 2, 1 dc in each of next 2 sc, rep

from * across. Ch 1, turn.

Row 3: Work 1 sc in each of next 2 dc, *ch 5, 1 sc in next ch-5 lp, ch 5, 1 sc in each of next 2 dc, rep from * across, working last sc in third ch of turning ch-3. Ch 2, turn.

Rep Rows 2 and 3 for pat st until piece measures same as grapevine strip from beg (about 53 inches).

Finishing: Sew the strips tog on the wrong side of the work with an overcast st (see Stitch Glossary), placing a grapevine strip on each outside edge and the remaining lace strips and grapevine strips alternating between.

Leaves: Make 24. With H hook and green, ch 6. Starting in second ch from hook, work 1 sc in each of next 4 ch, 3 sc in next ch, working along opposite edge of foundation ch, 1 sc in each of next 4 ch. Ch 1, turn. Working through back lps only, work 1 sc in each of next 5 sc, 3 sc in next sc, 1 sc in each of next 4 sc. Fasten off.

Vines: Make 24. With green and H hook, ch 36. Fasten off. Sew two leaves and two chains between each bunch of grapes as shown (see photo). Note that the positioning of the vine design alternates between each grape bunch, with the top and bottom vines being identical and the center one reversed.

Fringe: Cut 10-inch strands of black yarn and knot 3 in every other stitch along the short edges of the afghan. Trim the ends evenly.

☞ **Handwork Hints:** When changing colors along the back of the grape design, you can carry the black yarn loosely across the back of the grapes to save time. Clip and weave in the carried yarns after the strip has been completed.

₂₅ Lightning Strikes

Approximate finished size: 40 by 58 inches, including fringe

Rows of simple double crochet alternate with shaggy rows of cut yarn hooked into a filet mesh to make texture the main attraction of this off-white afghan. The afghan is worked in bulky yarn in three strips, with the lightning pattern extending from one strip to the next. If you wish, back this afghan with sturdy canvas and hang it on a wall—perfect for any contemporary interior.

Materials:

Reynolds Lopi, 100-gram (3.5-ounce) balls (bulky weight)
    18 balls color 51, off-white
Crochet hook, size K
Yarn needle

Gauge: 3 double crochet = 1 inch; 7 double-crochet rows = 5 inches

Strip No. 1 (left-hand strip): Ch 39.
Row 1: Starting in fourth ch from hook, work 1 dc in each ch across (37 dc, counting ch-2 at beg of row as 1 dc). Ch 2, turn.
Row 2: Skip first dc, work 1 dc through back lps only in each dc across. Ch 2, turn.
Work even in dc as now established for a total of 32 rows from beg. Ch 3 to turn at end of last row.
Filet-Mesh Section:
Row 1: (Turning ch-3 of previous row counts as 1 dc, ch 1 at beg of next row), skip first dc and next dc, *1 dc in next dc, ch 1, skip 1 dc, rep from * across, end 1 dc in second ch of turning ch-2. Ch 3, turn.
Row 2: Skip first dc and ch-1 sp, *1 dc in next dc, ch 1, rep from * across, end 1 dc in last dc, ch 3, turn.
Rows 3 through 8: Work as for Row 2. Ch 2 to turn at end of last row.
Row 9: Work 1 dc in first ch-1 sp, *1 dc in next dc, 1 dc in next ch-1 sp, rep from * across, end 1 dc in last dc. Ch 2, turn.
Row 10: Working through back lps only, work 1 dc in each dc across. Ch 2, turn.
Rows 11 through 16: Work as for Row 10.
Rep Rows 1 through 16 twice more. Fasten off.

Strip No. 2 (center strip): Ch 39. Work even in dc on 37 sts, referring to chart for mesh pat. Each row is shown on chart.

Strip No. 3 (right-hand strip): Ch. 39. Work even on 37 sts as follows: (8 rows dc through back lps only, 8 rows filet mesh) 3 times, end 32 rows dc through back lps only—80 rows.
Finishing: Sew the 3 strips tog with overcast st (see Stitch Glossary) with right side of work facing, carefully matching the rows.

Hooking: Cut 6-inch strands of yarn and knot 3 strands in each ch-1 sp in each filet mesh section.

Fringe: Knot six 6-inch strands of yarn in every third dc along the two short edges of the afghan.

☞ **Handwork Hints:** After sewing the strips together, make a finer match of the through-the-back-lps-only ridges by connecting them with a straight stitch that continues the ridge across the seam from strip to strip.

Strip No. 2 Stitch Chart

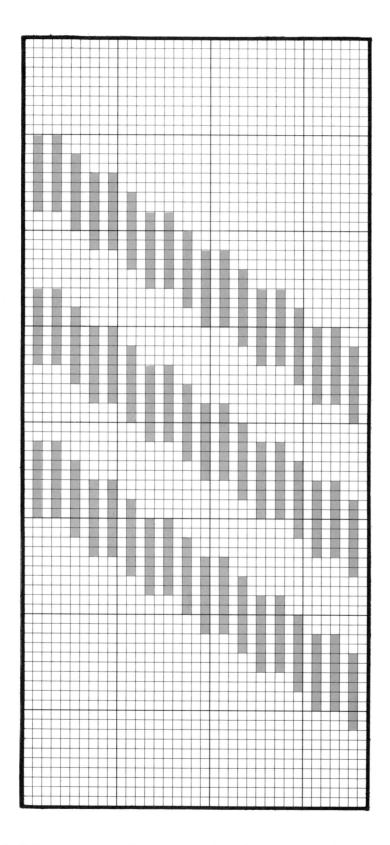

Stitch Key:

 Double crochet stitch (work into double crochet or chain-1 space on row below)

Chain-1 space (skip the double crochet or chain-1 space on row below)

105

²⁶ **Parrot**

Approximate finished size: 45 by 58 inches

Your parrot, cross-stitched in bright tropical colors, perches at the center of a sunny, yellow, afghan-stitch background. If you love doing cross-stitch embroidery, a restful pastime, hide the parrot deeper in the jungle with even more cross-stitched leaves. This afghan would also be stunning in black with the parrot worked in a light blue with yellow and shocking-pink highlights.

Materials:
Coats & Clark Red Heart Preference, 3.5-ounce skeins (knitting worsted weight)

   10 skeins color 231, yellow

Coats & Clark Red Heart Needlepoint and Crewel Yarn (3 strands, 12 yards):

   15 skeins color 559, green
   2 skeins color 742, bright blue
   1 skein color 010, red
   1 skein color 783, turquoise
   1 skein color 050, black

Afghan hook, size L

Crochet hook, size I

Yarn needle

Gauge: 7 stitches = 2 inches; 3 rows = 1 inch

Pattern Stitch:
Make a chain of the specified length.

Row 1: First half: Ch 1, insert hook in the second ch from hook, yo and draw through, *insert hook in the next ch, yo and draw through, rep from * across. *Second half:* Yo and draw through first lp on hook, *yo and draw through 2 lps on hook, rep from * across.

Row 2: First half: Ch 1, skip first vertical bar, *insert hook from right to left under top strand of next vertical bar, yo and draw through, rep from * across, ending by inserting hook under both strands of last vertical bar, yo and draw through. *Second half:* Yo and draw through first lp on hook, *yo and draw through 2 lps on hook, rep from * across.

Rep Row 2 for pat.

Strips: Make 3. With afghan hook and yellow, ch 46. Work even in pat st for 156 rows. Fasten off.

Finishing: Place two strips side by side, and, using I hook and yellow, begin to join by making a sl st on the hook. Then, starting from the bottom, *insert hook from right to left through corresponding first vertical bars on the edge of each strip along the seamline, yo and draw through two vertical bars and through lp on hook, rep from *, working up the seam on each successive pair of sts along each side of seam and being careful not to pull sts too tight. When seam has been completed, fasten off and rep to join remaining strip. Work 4 rows of yellow sc around entire piece, working 3 sc in each corner, and join with a sl st to first sc. Then, with yellow, work 1 row of reverse sc (work as for sc but work from left to right instead of right to left) around the entire piece and join with a sl st to the first st. Fasten off.

Embroidery: Centering the design on the joined afghan,

work cross-stitch embroidery (see Stitch Glossary) in the colors shown on chart, using stem st (see Stitch Glossary) as indicated for the parrot's beak and face.

☞ **Handwork Hints:** Before beginning the cross-stitching, be sure that the parrot is centered properly and then outline each of his color areas in cross-stitch. Once this is finished, you can relax and fill in the areas without having to refer constantly to the chart. When following a complicated chart such as this one, you may find that using a ruler will help you keep your place. Another way to facilitate the work is to baste in the outline of the broad free-form areas, such as the leaves, with a contrasting color of thread, fill in with the proper color of cross-stitch, and then remove your guideline. This method will work wherever the stitches need not be exactly placed.

Embroidery Chart

Note: Embroidery extends over 121 stitches by 136 rows.

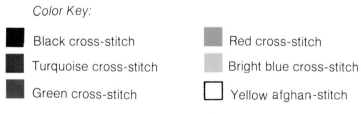

Color Key:

Black cross-stitch   Red cross-stitch

Turquoise cross-stitch   Bright blue cross-stitch

Green cross-stitch   Yellow afghan-stitch

---- Black stem stitch

109

²⁷ Motifs Ahoy

Approximate finished size: 53 by 64 inches

Experienced Crocheters Only

A nautical feeling is evoked by this afghan, thanks to steering-wheel and life-preserver motifs, trimmed with a thick, twisted cord. Use it as shown here for a netlike decorative effect appropriate as a wall hanging in a beach house or on a boat, or line it with a contrasting color of fabric, such as a light blue or red sailcloth, and use it as a coverlet.

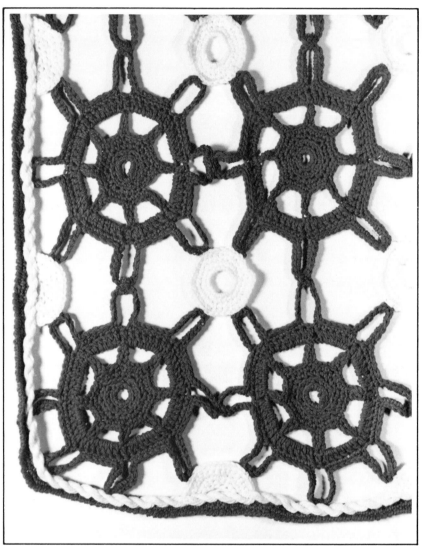

Materials:
Coats & Clark Red Heart Preference, 100-gram (3.5-ounce) skeins (knitting worsted weight)
    8 skeins color 846, skipper blue
    3 skeins color 4, cream
Crochet hook, size H
Yarn needle
7 yards off-white twisted cord, ½ inch in diameter

Gauge: One life-preserver motif = 3¼ inches in diameter

Note: On all the following rnds, end the rnd by joining with a sl st to the first st and ch 1 unless otherwise specified.

Life-Preserver Motifs: Make 20. With cream, ch 12, join with sl st to form a ring.
Rnd 1: Work 18 sc in ring.
Rnd 2: *Work 1 sc in each of next 2 sc, 2 sc in next sc, rep from * around (24 sc).
Rnd 3: *Work 1 sc in each of next 3 sc, 2 sc in next sc, rep from * around (30 sc).
Rnd 4: *Work 1 sc in each of next 4 sc, 2 sc in next sc, rep from * around (36 sc). Join with sl st to first st. Fasten off.

Life-Preserver Half-Motifs: Make 18. With white, ch 8.
Row 1: Starting in second ch from hook, work *1 sc in each of next 2 ch, 2 sc in next ch, rep from * once more, end 1 sc in last ch (9 sc). Ch 1, turn.
Row 2: *Work 2 sc in next sc, 1 sc in each of next 3 sc, rep from * once more, end 2 sc in last sc (12 sc). Ch 1, turn.
Row 3: *Work 2 sc in next sc, 1 sc in each of next 4 sc, rep from * once more, end 2 sc in next sc, 1 sc in last sc (15 sc). Ch 1, turn.
Row 4: *Work 2 sc in next sc, 1 sc in each of next 5 sc, rep from * once more, end 2 sc in next sc, 1 sc in each of next 2 sc (18 sc). Fasten off.

Steering-Wheel Motifs: Make 30. With blue, ch 6. Join with sl st to form a ring.
Rnd 1: Work 12 sc in ring.
Rnd 2: Working in back lps only, *work 1 sc in next sc, 2 sc in next sc, rep from * around (18 sc).
Rnd 3: Working in back lps only, *work 1 sc in each of next 2 sc, 2 sc in next sc, rep from * around (24 sc).
Rnd 4: Working through both lps, *work 1 sc in each of next 3 sc, ch 4, turn. Starting in second ch from hook, work 1 sc in each of next 3 ch, 1 sc in same st as last sc preceding the ch-3, rep from * around (8 spokes). Join with sl st to first st. Fasten off.
Rnd 5: Join yarn in tip of any spoke, work 1 sc in same tip, *ch 6, work 1 sc in tip of next spoke, rep from * around, end

ch 6, join with sl st to first st. Ch 2.

Rnd 6: *Work 6 dc in next ch-6 lp, 1 dc in next sc, rep from * around, end 6 dc in next ch-6 lp. Join with sl st to second ch of starting ch-2.

Rnd 7: Work (1 sc, ch 11, 1 sc) in second ch of starting ch-2, *1 sc in each of next 6 dc, (1 sc, ch 11, 1 sc) in next dc, rep from * around, end 1 sc in each of next 6 dc (8 ch-11 lps). Join with sl st to first st.

Rnd 8: *Work 13 sc in next ch-11 lp, skip next sc at base of ch-11 lp, 1 sl st in each of next 6 sc, skip next sc at base of ch-11 lp, rep from * around. Join with sl st to first st. Fasten off.

Finishing: Lay out the steering-wheel motifs in a five by six arrangement. Following diagram A for placement, position one of the life-preservers between each set of four motifs and then position the half-life-preservers along the outside edges as shown. Now using blue yarn, overcast (see Stitch Glossary) the motifs together on the wrong side of the work, sewing through the center 3 sc at the tip of each spoke and matching these 3 sc with the center 3 sc of another spoke. The shaded portions on diagram B indicate which of the 36 sc on the outside edge of the life-preserver should be sewn to an adjoining spoke. The remaining sc should be left free. When all the pieces have been joined, work the border.

Border: With blue, join the yarn in any corner spoke, *ch 12, work 1 sc in each of center 3 sc at tip of next spoke, ch 12 to next half-life-preserver, work 1 sc in the end of each of the 4 rnds of the first part of the motif, ch 4, 1 sc in the end of each of the 4 rnds of the second part of the motif, rep from * across to the end of the half-life-preserver preceding the spoke before the next corner spoke, (ch 12 to next spoke, 3 sc in each of center 3 sc at tip of spoke) 3 times, rep from * along each remaining side, working around each corner as instructed and completing first corner to correspond to the other three corners. Now work 2 rnds of sc around, working 1 sc in each ch or sc on the first rnd and 1 sc in each sc on the next rnd. Finally, work 1 rnd of reverse sc (work as for sc but work from left to right instead of from right to left) around the entire piece. Fasten off. Sew the twisted cord along the inside edge of the border. Block.

☞ **Handwork Hints:** The joining of the various motifs can be confusing. You might like to make an actual-size tracing of a few of the motifs in the joined position to be certain that you are joining the spokes and life-preservers in the proper places.

Diagram A

Leave four corner steering-wheel motifs free as shown here.

Top row of steering-wheel motifs

Repeat this row of steering-wheel motifs 4 times; then join remaining steering-wheel motifs to correspond to top row.

Diagram B

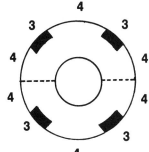

Key:
Each number: Number of single-crochet stitches on outside edge of life preserver
---- Half-life-preserver

28 Colonial Ripples

Approximate finished size: 49 by 60 inches

No Experience Needed

The perfect beginner's project and as traditional as can be, this rippled afghan features warm, fall shades of gold to blend with any colonial or country decor. If you decide to change the colors, think in terms of using four shades of the same color to get the desired ripple effect.

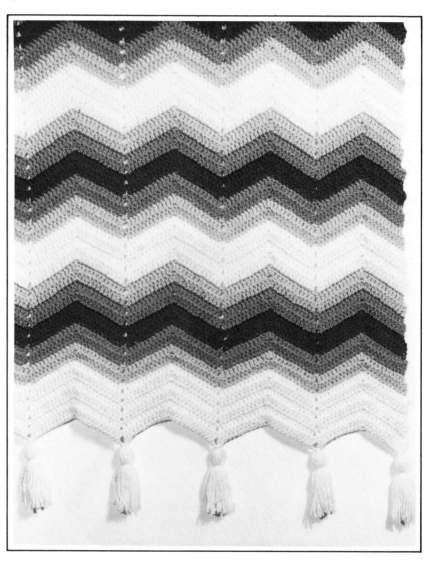

Materials:
Phildar Leader, 100-gram (3.5-ounce) balls (sport weight)
     4 balls color 52, pastel yellow (A)
     3 balls color 44, gold (B)
     3 balls color 89, saffran (C)
     2 balls color 50, horsechestnut (D)
Crochet hook, size G
Yarn needle

Gauge: 25 stitches = 6 inches; 8 rows = 5 inches

Pattern Stitch:
Make a chain of the specified length.
Row 1: Ch 2, work 1 dc in third ch from hook, 1 dc in each of next 10 ch, *3 dc in next ch, 1 dc in each of next 11 ch, skip 2 ch, 1 dc in each of next 11 ch, rep from * across to within last 12 ch, end 3 dc in next ch, 1 dc in each of next 11 ch. Ch 2, turn.
Row 2: Working through back lps only, skip first dc, *1 dc in each of next 11 dc, 3 dc in next dc, 1 dc in each of next 11 dc, skip 2 dc, rep from * across, ending last rep as follows on last 12 sts: 1 dc in each of next 10 dc, skip 1 dc, 1 dc through both lps of last dc. Ch 2, turn. Rep Row 2 for pat st.

Strips: Make 2. With A, ch 98. Working in pat st throughout, work in color pat of 6 rows A, (2 rows B, 2 rows C, 2 rows D, 2 rows C, 2 rows B, 4 rows A) 6 times, ending 2 rows A. Fasten off.

Finishing: Sew strips tog on wrong side of work with overcast st (see Stitch Glossary), being careful to match stripes.

Tassels: Make 17. Cut twenty 9-inch strands of color A and tie in the center with a 7-inch strand. Fold the strands in half at the tie, wrap one end of one of the strands securely around the folded strands 1 inch below the tie, fasten off, and trim the ends evenly. Sew one tassel to each point along the top and bottom edges of the afghan.

☞ **Handwork Hints:** You may wish to work this afghan in one piece to avoid seaming. If so, ch 198 to start and work the color pattern as outlined in the instructions.

Blue Willow

Approximate finished size: 46 by 61 inches

Three strips of textured crochet are seamed together to form the background for an overall embroidered scene reminiscent of the familiar blue-and-white china painted with Oriental-style weeping willow and curved bridge.

Materials:

Phildar Pegase 206, 50-gram (1¾-ounce) balls (knitting worsted weight)

  20 balls color 10, blanc (white)
  4 balls color 82, roy (blue)

Crochet hook, size I

Yarn needle

Gauge in Pattern Stitch: 3 stitches = 1 inch

Pattern Stitch:

Row 1: Work 1 sc in second ch from hook, *1 dc in next ch, 1 sc in next ch, rep from * across. Ch 2, turn.

Row 2: Work 1 dc in each sc and 1 sc in each dc. Ch 1 to turn if the row ends with 1 dc, ch 2 to turn if row ends with 1 sc. Rep Row 2 for pattern.

Strips: Make 3. With white, ch 42. Work pat on 41 sts until piece measures 58 inches from beg. Fasten off.

Finishing: Sew the three strips tog with an overcast st (see Stitch Glossary). With white, work 1 rnd of sc around edge, working 3 sc in each corner. Fasten off. *Next Rnd:* With blue, attach yarn in any center corner st and work 1 sc in each of next 2 sts, *(1 sc, ch 2, 1 sc) in next st, 1 sc in each of next 5 sts, rep from * around, working 3 sc in each corner and working fewer or more sc as necessary in order to begin and end each of the four sides with 2 sc before and after the center corner st with (1 sc, ch 2, 1 sc) in next adjacent st. Fasten off.

Embroidery: Enlarge embroidery diagram (see "Handwork Hints") and complete embroidery with blue yarn. Work all outlines in stem stitch and all shaded areas in long and short stitch (see Stitch Glossary).

☞ **Handwork Hints:** To enlarge the embroidery pattern, tape sheets of tracing paper together to make a piece large enough to accommodate the actual size of the pattern as indicated on the diagram. Divide into the same number of squares as there are on the chart, and then, square by square, copy the pattern on the tracing paper. Transfer the embroidery pattern to the afghan with long basting stitches worked through the tissue. Carefully tear away the paper and embroider along the basting stitches.

Embroidery Diagram

Each square = 1 inch

㉚ Crayon Stripes

Approximate finished size: 46 by 59 inches

No Experience Needed

Just one look at this sunny, full-size afghan and spirits soar. Bright-colored strips in double crochet with pinstripes of white single crochet placed between create a crisp effect when finished with a border of brilliant emerald green single crochet all around. To neaten the look further, crocheted chains are sewn over the seams. If you weave in the yarn ends carefully enough when finished, you'll have a completely reversible blanket.

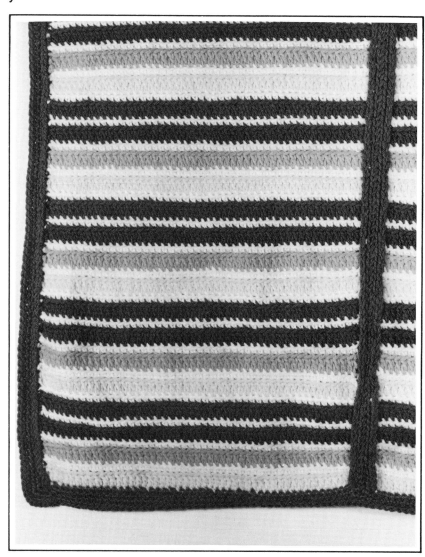

Materials:
Coats & Clark Red Heart Preference, 100-gram (3.5-ounce) skeins

- 3 skeins color 01, white
- 3 skeins color 676, emerald
- 2 skeins color 257, tangerine
- 2 skeins color 846, skipper blue
- 2 skeins color 231, yellow

Crochet hook, size J

Yarn needle

Gauge: 7 double crochet = 2 inches; (1 row double crochet, 1 row single crochet) = 1 inch

Pattern Stitch:
Row 1: Starting in third ch from hook, work 1 dc in each ch across, counting turning ch at beg of row as 1 dc. Fasten off.
Row 2: Return to beg of row, join next color in first dc. Work even in sc through back lps only. Fasten off.
Row 3: Return to beg of row, join next color in first sc. Ch 2 (counts as 1 dc) and work even in dc through back lps only across. Fasten off.
Rep Rows 2 and 3 for pat.

Strips: Make 3. With yellow, ch 52. Work even in pat st, working all sc rows in white and changing the color of each dc row in sequence as follows: yellow, tangerine, emerald, blue. Repeat the sequence 14 times in all and end with 1 row of yellow dc.

Finishing: Work 1 row of emerald sc around each strip and sew the strips tog with overcast st (see Stitch Glossary). Work 3 rows of emerald sc around entire joined piece. Make 6 chains, each long enough to cover the overcast seams. Sew one chain on either side of the two seams and one chain over the first row of emerald sc on each of the two long outside edges.

☞ **Handwork Hints:** The beginner will learn the real meaning of the word "finishing" with this piece. Some of the yarn ends at the end of each row can be covered when working the emerald sc around the outside edge of each strip. Hold the yarn ends along the edge you are working on and crochet over them. Be careful not to work too many ends in at once or the edge will become too bulky. Weave the remaining ends through several stitches on the wrong side of the work and trim them close to the piece.

CROCHETED LAP ROBES

③① Navajo Symbols

Approximate finished size: 39 by 50 inches

Authentic Navajo symbols adorn the strips of this single-crocheted lap robe worked in gray, black, and red on a white background. It is starkly geometric, yet it has a woven look resulting from the changing of the colors. If you'd like a more sharply defined edge around the symbols and along the stripes, you could sew on black crocheted chains or embroider chain stitches along the outlines.

Materials:
Knitting worsted, 4-ounce skeins
    5 skeins white
    2 skeins black
    1 skein gray
    1 skein red
Crochet hook, size J
Yarn needle

Gauge: 8 stitches = 3 inches; 3 rows = 1 inch

Strips: For each strip, ch 106. Starting in second ch from hook, work even in sc on 105 sts, working color designs as specified on the corresponding charts for Strips No. 1 and No. 2 and completing Strip No. 3 as specified below.

Strip No. 1: Make 1. Work chart to completion. Fasten off.

Strip No. 2: Make 2. Work chart to completion. Fasten off.

Strip No. 3: Make 2. Work 2 rows white, 2 rows black, 2 rows gray, 2 rows black, 14 rows white, 2 rows black, 2 rows gray, 2 rows black, 2 rows white. Fasten off.

Finishing: With white, sew the strips tog on the wrong side with an overcast st (see Stitch Glossary), placing the No. 1 strip in the center, a No. 3 strip on either side of it, and a No. 2 strip on each outside edge (see photo). Finish the outside edge of each No. 2 strip with 2 rows sc in black, 2 rows gray, and 2 rows black. Fasten off. Work 1 row of color-over-color sc along each long edge of piece.

Fringe: Cut 10-inch strands of black yarn and knot 6 strands in every third st along each short edge.

☞ **Handwork Hints:** When working with two colors on one row, work the single crochet over the thread not in use. On the rows where three colors are used, the unused yarn must be cut and the ends woven in later, as only one strand of yarn should be carried under the working color at a time. Also, to change colors from one single-crochet stitch to another, work the old color up to the point where two loops remain on the hook, remove them with the new color, and proceed to work the next stitch in the new color for as many stitches as specified.

Strip No. 1

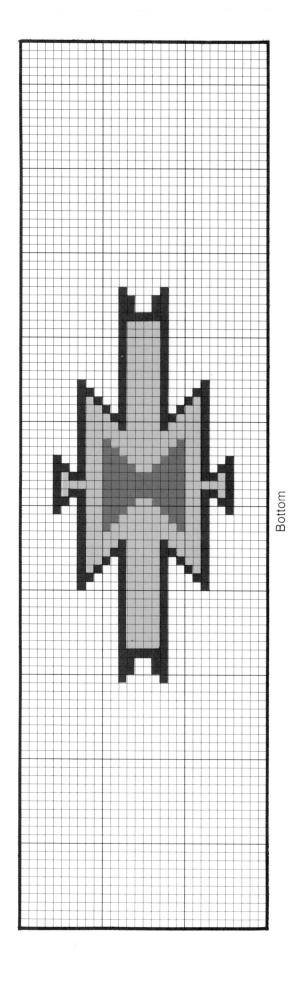

Bottom

124

Strip No. 2

Color Key:

☐ White

■ Black

▨ Red

▨ Gray

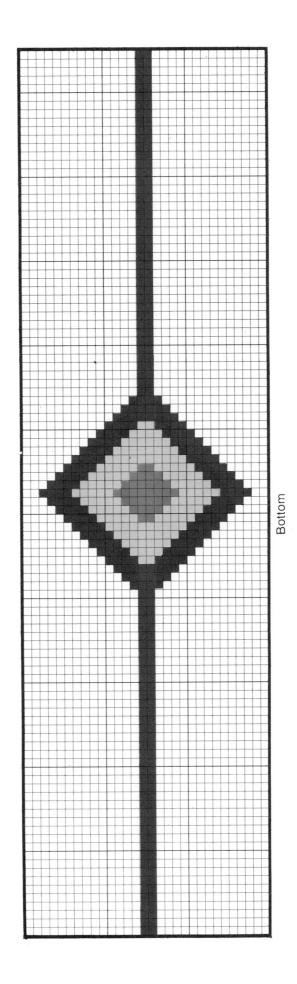

Bottom

₃₂ Portable Lap Robe

Approximate finished size: 42 by 45 inches

No Experience Needed

Textured stitches stripe this lap robe made with bulky tweed yarn, but the real novelty lies in the fact that it can be folded and carried like a bag by means of its own crocheted handles. With enough room inside the "bag" to carry a pillow, this lap robe will make an ideal gift for travelers who often find themselves on chilly airplanes with no blankets or pillows in sight or for the football or soccer fan.

Materials:
Reynolds Icelandic Homespun, 1¾-ounce balls (knitting worsted weight)

      10 balls color 410, dark brown

      10 balls color 401, off-white

Crochet hook, size K

Yarn needle

Button, 1⅜ inches in diameter

Gauge: 13 double crochet = 5 inches; 3 rows = 2 inches

Note: Work with one strand of off-white and one strand of dark brown together throughout.

Note: To work Front Post dc (FPdc), work as for dc, but instead of inserting hook into st, insert hook from front to back to front around vertical post of dc on row below. To work Back-Post dc (BPdc), work as for FPdc, but insert hook from back to front to back around post of dc of row below.

Right Panel:
Row 1: Ch 29. Starting in fourth ch from hook, work 1 dc in each ch across (27 dc, counting ch-2 at beg of each row as 1 dc). Ch 2, turn.

Row 2: Skip first dc, work 1 dc in each dc across. Ch 2, turn.

Row 3: Skip first dc, work (1 FPdc around next st, 1 dc in each of next 3 sts) 3 times, 1 FPdc around next st, 1 dc in each of remaining 13 dc across. Ch 2, turn.

Row 4: Skip first dc, work 1 dc in each of next 12 sts, (1 BPdc around next st, 1 dc in each of next 3 sts) 3 times, 1 BPdc around next st, 1 dc in second ch of turning ch-2 of previous row. Ch 2, turn.

Rep Rows 3 and 4 until piece measures 44 inches from beg. End by working 2 rows of dc. Fasten off.

Left Panel: Work as for right panel, but reverse positioning of sts (start with 13 dc and then work post dc section).

Center Panel: Ch 56. Starting in fourth ch from hook, work 2 rows of dc on 54 sts (counting ch-2 at beg of each row as 1 dc). Ch 2 to turn at end of each row.

Row 3: Skip first dc, (1 FPdc around next st, 1 dc in each of next 3 sts) 3 times, 1 FPdc around next st, 1 dc in each of next 26 dc, (1 FPdc around next st, 1 dc in each of next 3 sts) 3 times, 1 FPdc around next st, 1 dc in last st. Ch 2, turn.

Row 4: Skip first dc, (work 1 BPdc around next st, 1 dc in each of next 3 sts) 3 times, 1 BPdc around next st, 1 dc in each of next 26 dc, (1 BPdc around next st, 1 dc in each of next 3 sts) 3 times, 1 BPdc in next st, 1 dc in last st. Ch 2, turn.

Rep Rows 3 and 4 until piece measures 44 inches from beg.

End by working 2 rows of dc. Fasten off.

Finishing: Pieces will be joined so that the post dc section of the right and left panels are positioned on the outside edge of the blanket. With right sides together, join the left panel to the center panel by working 1 row of sc with a ch-1 between each 2 sc and working through both thicknesses. Join the right panel in the same manner. Work 1 row of sc around, working 3 sc in each corner.

Handles: Make 2. Working with 2 strands of each color, ch 71. Work even in sc on 70 sts for 3 rows. Sl st across short end of piece, work 1 row of sc along foundation-ch edge of strip, and sl st across next short end. Fasten off.

Button Tab: Still working with 2 strands of each color, ch 6, work even in sc on 5 sts for 22 rows, ch 1 to turn at end of each row. To shape buttonhole, work 1 sc in each of first 2 sts, ch 1, skip 1 st, 1 sc in each of next 2 sts. Ch 1, turn, 1 sc in each of first 2 sts, 1 sc in ch-1 sp, 1 sc in each of last 2 sts—buttonhole completed. Ch 1, turn. Work 1 more row of sc. Work 1 row of sc with ch-1 between each sc around piece, working 3 sc in each corner. Fasten off.

Positioning of Handles and Tab: Lay the piece flat with right side down, fold the right and left panels to the center of the blanket, fold the two short edges of the center panel to the center, and then fold it in half once again. Position the tab and handles as shown in the photo and sew them in place with the yarn needle and double yarn. Sew the button in place to correspond to the buttonhole.

☞ **Handwork Hints:** Whenever you need to work with two strands of yarn held together, spend some time winding balls of the combined yarns—this will help prevent tangling and make the work go faster.

Stitch Sampler

Approximate finished size: 45 by 45 inches

A delightful variety of pattern stitches is used in the eight-inch squares made for this lap robe in orange blossom yarn. This one is designed especially for crocheters who get restless repeating the same design over and over. Using one color only heightens the effect of the varying textures.

Materials:
Pingouin Pingochamp, 100-gram (3.5-ounce) skeins (knitting worsted weight)
    8 skeins color 306, orange blossom
Crochet hook, size G
Yarn needle

Gauge:
    Square No. 1: 4 double crochet = 1 inch
    Square No. 2: 2 pattern stitches = 1 inch
    Square No. 3: 1 pattern stitch = 1 inch
    Square No. 4: 5 pattern stitches = 3 inches
    Square No. 5: 2 pattern stitches = 3 inches

Square No. 1: Make 5. Ch 37.
Row 1: Starting in ninth ch from hook, work *1 dc in each of next 5 ch, ch 2, skip 2 ch, rep from * across, end 1 dc in last ch. Ch 5, turn.
Row 2: Work *1 dc in first dc of 5-dc group, (ch 1, skip 1 dc, 1 dc in next dc) twice, ch 2, rep from * across, end 1 dc in third ch of turning ch-5. Ch 5, turn.
Row 3: Work *(1 dc in next dc, 1 dc in next ch-1 sp) twice, 1 dc in next dc, ch 2, rep from * across, end 1 dc in third ch of turning ch-5. Ch 5, turn.
Rep Rows 2 and 3 for pat st until piece measures 8 inches from beg. Fasten off.

Square No. 2: Make 6. Ch 33.
Row 1: Insert hook in third ch from hook, *yo, draw through, skip 1 ch, insert hook in next ch, yo, draw through, (yo, draw through 2 lps on hook) twice, ch 1, insert hook in same ch as last st, rep from * across, end yo, draw through, skip 1 ch, insert hook in last ch, yo, draw through (yo, draw through 2 lps on hook) twice, sc in same ch as last st. Ch 2, turn.
Row 2: Insert hook in last sc of previous row, yo, draw through, *insert hook in next ch-1 sp, yo, draw through, (yo, draw through 2 lps on hook) twice, ch 1, insert hook in same ch-1 sp as last st, yo, draw through, rep from * across, end insert hook in second ch of turning ch-2, yo, draw through, (yo, draw through 2 lps on hook) twice, 1 sc in same ch. Ch 2, turn.
Rep Row 2 for pat st until piece measures 8 inches from beg. Fasten off.

Square No. 3: Make 4. Ch 34.
Row 1: Starting in second ch from hook, work 1 sc, *ch 2, skip 3 ch, (2 dc, ch 1, 2 dc) in next ch, ch 2, skip 3 ch, 1 sc in next ch, rep from * across. Ch 6, turn.
Row 2: Work *(2 dc, ch 1, 2 dc) in next ch-1 sp, ch 3, rep from *across, end (2 dc, ch 1, 2 dc) in last ch-1 sp, ch 1, 1 tr in sc of first row. Ch 1, turn.

Row 3: Work 1 sc in tr, ch 2, *(2 dc, ch 1, 2 dc) in next ch-1 sp, ch 2, 1 sc in next ch-3 sp, ch 2, rep from * across, end (2 dc, ch 1, 2 dc) in next ch-1 sp, ch 2, 1 sc in fifth ch of turning ch-6. Ch 6, turn.
Rep Rows 2 and 3 for pat st until piece measures 8 inches from beg. Fasten off.

Square No. 4: Make 6. Ch 27 loosely.
Row 1: Starting in second ch from hook, work *(1 sc, ch 1, 1 sc) in ch, skip 1 ch, rep from * across, end 1 sc in last ch. Ch 1, turn.
Row 2: Work *(1 sc, ch 1, 1 sc) in first sc of next 3-st group, rep from * across, end 1 sc in last st. Ch 1, turn.
Rep Row 2 for pat st until piece measures 8 inches from beg.

Square No. 5: Make 4. Ch 37.
Row 1: Work 1 sc in tenth ch from hook, *(ch 3, 1 sl st in first ch—picot made), ch 3, skip 2 ch, 1 dc in next ch, ch 3, skip 2 ch, 1 sc in next ch, rep from * across, end picot, ch 3, 1 dc in last ch. Ch 3, turn.
Row 2: Work 1 dc in next ch-3 sp, *ch 5, 1 dc in next ch-3 sp, 1 dc in next dc, 1 dc in next ch-3 sp, rep from * across, end ch 5, 1 dc in last ch-sp, 1 dc in fourth ch, counting from last sc of previous row. Ch 6, turn.
Row 3: *Work 1 sc in next ch-5 sp, picot, ch 3, 1 dc in second dc of next 3-dc group, ch 3, rep from * across, end 1 sc in last ch-5 sp, picot, ch 3, 1 dc in third ch of turning ch-3. Ch 3, turn.
Rep Rows 2 and 3 for pat st until piece measures 8 inches from beg. Fasten off.

Finishing: Work 1 row of sc around each square, working 31 sc along each edge and 3 sc in each corner. Referring to placement diagram, sew squares tog on wrong side of work with an overcast st (see Stitch Glossary and "Handwork Hints" with Flowers at the Crossroads, p. 96.) Work 2 rows of sc around outside edge of joined piece, working 3 sc in each corner.

Picot Edging: Starting in center st of any corner, ch 3, picot (see Square No. 5), ch 1, 1 dc in next st, *ch 1, skip 1 st, 1 dc in next st, picot, rep from * to the 3 sts worked in next corner, ch 1, work 1 dc in first st of corner, (picot, ch 1, 1 dc in next st) twice, picot, work along remaining three sides of piece as now established, working the next two corners in same manner. To join rnd, work 1 dc in first st of starting corner, picot, ch 1, sl st to third ch of starting ch-3. Fasten off.

☞ **Handwork Hints:** Before working each square, test the gauge. Using Square No. 1 as your guide, work the remaining squares on a larger or smaller hook, if necessary,

Placement Diagram

5	4	1	2	3
2	5	4	1	2
1	2	3	4	5
4	1	2	3	4
3	4	5	2	1

to match it in size. Don't worry about a difference of ½ inch or less, for the single-crochet edging should even out the squares when they are joined stitch to stitch.

CROCHETED BABY BLANKETS

³⁴ Fiesta

Approximate finished size: 30 by 43 inches

No Experience Needed

Layer upon layer of bright orange, yellow, and blue ruffles outline this Latin-inspired baby blanket, which has also been appliqued with big crocheted balloons to heighten its carnival mood. Its oval shape makes it ideal as a decorative throw for the nursery floor as well as for a crib; simply sew on a heavy canvas backing first.

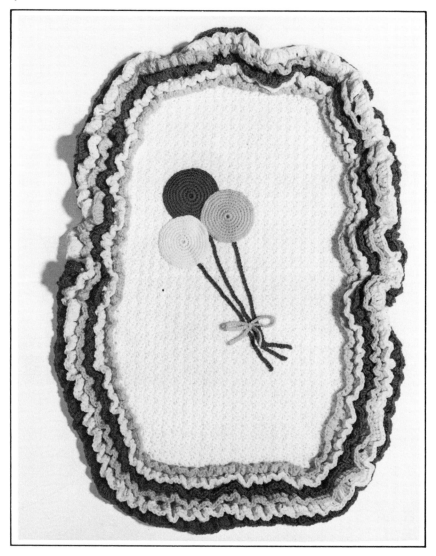

Materials:
Coats & Clark Red Heart 4-ply handknitting yarn, 3.5-ounce skeins

    2 skeins color 3, off-white
    2 skeins color 257, tangerine
    2 skeins color 231, yellow
    2 skeins color 846, skipper blue

Crochet hook, size J

Gauge in Pattern Stitch: 8 stitches = 3 inches; 7 rows = 3 inches

Note: To inc 1 st, work 2 sts in same st; to dec 1 st, skip 1 st.

Pattern Stitch:
Row 1: Work 1 sc in second ch from hook, *1 dc in next ch, 1 sc in next ch, rep from * across. Ch 1 to turn if row ends with 1 dc; ch 2 if row ends with 1 sc. Turn.
Row 2: Work 1 dc in each sc and 1 sc in each dc across. Ch 1 to turn if row ends with 1 dc; ch 2 if row ends with 1 sc. Turn.

Background Piece: With off-white yarn, ch 32 loosely. Work first row of pat st. Keeping to pat, inc 1 st at each edge every other row 8 times in all (47 sts). Work even for 16 inches. Dec 1 st at each edge on every other row 8 times (31 sts). Work 1 row even. Work 1 row of sc around entire piece, working enough sts so that work lies flat. Fasten off.

Ruffled Edge:
Rnd 1: With orange, work 4 tr in every other sc around edge of main piece, chaining 4 to count as first tr of rnd, join with sl st to fourth ch of starting ch-4.
Rnd 2: Working in back of previous row, ch 3, work sl st around base of fourth tr of first 4-tr group, *ch 3, work sl st around base of fourth tr of next 4-tr group, rep from * around, join with sl st to first ch of rnd. Fasten off.
Rnd 3: With yellow, work 5 tr in each ch-3 lp around, chaining 4 to count as first tr of rnd, join with sl st to fourth ch of starting ch-4.
Rnd 4: Continuing with yellow, rep Rnd 2. Fasten off.
Rnd 5: With blue, work as for Rnd 3.
Rnd 6: With blue, work as for Rnd 4, but work ch-4 lps instead of ch-3 lps. Fasten off.
Rnd 7: With orange, work as for Rnd 3.
Rnd 8: With orange, work as for Rnd 6. Fasten off.
Rnd 9: With yellow, work as for Rnd 3, but work 6 tr in each lp.
Rnd 10: With yellow, work as for Rnd 6, but work ch-5 lps instead of ch-4 lps. Fasten off.
Rnd 11: With blue, work as for Rnd 9. Fasten off.

Balloons: Make 1 each in yellow, blue, and tangerine. Ch 4, join with sl st to form a ring. Work 10 sc in ring. Working in rnds, *work 2 sc in next st, 1 sc in next st, rep from * around until piece measures 4 inches in diameter. Join with sl st and fasten off.

Strings: Make 3. With blue, ch 50.

Bow: With orange, ch 70. Tie into a bow.

Finishing: Arrange balloons, strings, and bow as shown in photo. Sew in place.

☞ **Handwork Hints:** Attaching the appliquéd balloons with sewing thread rather than yarn will make the joining smooth and unnoticeable.

Pandas on Parade

Approximate finished size: 30 by 43 inches

On a background as green as that of their favorite food, bamboo shoots, three big pandas (crocheted separately and appliquéd in different poses) frolic to delight baby and anyone else who passes by. Of course, there's no reason to stop with just three pandas—cover the blanket with them! Then, go on to make another panda to be framed as a picture and another to adorn a coordinating pillow with the same bamboo-leaf green background.

Materials:
Knitting worsted, 4-ounce skeins
    5 skeins green
    1 skein black
    1 skein white
Crochet hooks, sizes K and H
Yarn needle

Gauge: 3 stitches = 1 inch; 2 rows = 1 inch

Strips: Make 3. With green and K hook, ch 30.
Row 1: Ch 2, (1 sc, 2 dc) in third ch from hook, *skip 2 ch, (1 sc, 2 dc) in next ch, rep from * across row, ending 1 sc in last ch. Ch 1, turn.
Row 2: *(1 sc, 2 dc) in next sc, skip 2 dc, rep from * across row, ending 1 sc in last sc. Ch 1, turn.
Rep Row 2 for pat st until strip measures 43 inches from beg. Fasten off.

Finishing: With K hook and green, work 1 row of sc around each of the three crocheted strips, working 3 sc in each corner. Sew strips tog on wrong side of work with overcast st (see Stitch Glossary) through back lps only of sc edging.

Fringe: Cut 7-inch strands of green yarn. Knot 3 strands in every other st around entire outside edge of blanket.

Three Pandas: Use H hook throughout.
Head: Make 3. With white, ch 4, join with sl st to form a ring. *Rnd 1:* Ch 1, work 8 sc in ring, join with sl st to first st. *Rnd 2:* *Work 1 sc in first sc, 2 sc in next sc, rep from * around (12 sts), join with sl st to first st. *Rnd 3:* Work as for Rnd 2 (18 sts). *Rnd 4:* Work as for Rnd 2 (27 sts). Fasten off.

Body: Make 3. With white, work as for head for 5 rnds (40 sts). *Rnd 6:* Work 2 sc in every third sc (53 sts). Fasten off.

Muzzle: Make 3. With white, ch 4. *Rnd 1:* Work 3 sc in second ch from hook, 1 sc in next ch, 3 sc in next ch, turn work to opposite edge of foundation ch, work 1 sc in next st. *Rnd 2:* Work 1 sc in first st of previous rnd, 3 sc in next st, 1 sc in each of next 3 sc, 3 sc in next st, join with sl st to next st. Fasten off.

Eye patches: Make 6. With black, ch 3, join with sl st to form a ring. *Rnd 1:* Work (1 hdc, 3 dc, 1 hdc, 3 sc) in ring, join with sl st to first st. Fasten off.

Ears: Make 6. With black, work as for Rnds 1 and 2 of head. *Rnd 3:* Work in sc without inc around, join with sl st to first st. Fasten off.

Legs: Make 6. With black, ch 26. *Rnd 1:* Starting in second ch from hook, *work 1 sc in ch, 2 sc in next ch, rep from * across, work 2 more sc in last ch; working along opposite edge of foundation ch, *(insert hook in next ch and pull up a lp) twice, yo, draw through all 3 lps on hook, rep from * across, 2 more sc in last ch of rnd. *Rnd 2:* Work 1 sc in each of next sc to within last 3 sc on this side of rnd, work 1 sc in each of last 3 sc, work 1 sc in each st along inner curve of piece to first dc of this rnd, work 1 sc in each dc, join with sl st to next st. Fasten off.

Panda Finishing: Referring to the illustration for placement of ears, eye patches, and muzzle, assemble each head and attach the pieces with sewing thread. Then with black yarn and the yarn needle, embroider a satin-stitch nose and straight-stitch mouth (see Stitch Glossary), as shown on the illustration. With white yarn and the yarn needle, make one French knot on each eye patch as shown. Assemble the parts of the panda on the blanket in the poses shown in the photo or create your own and sew in place with matching thread.

☞ **Handwork Hints:** When you tack the parts of each panda together in the desired pose, attach them firmly before sewing the panda to the blanket. In this way, you will need to sew only around the outer edge of the joined panda, so that the amount of stitching showing on the wrong side of the work will be minimal. Be sure to sew the appliqués on securely so that none of the small pieces will fall into baby's hands.

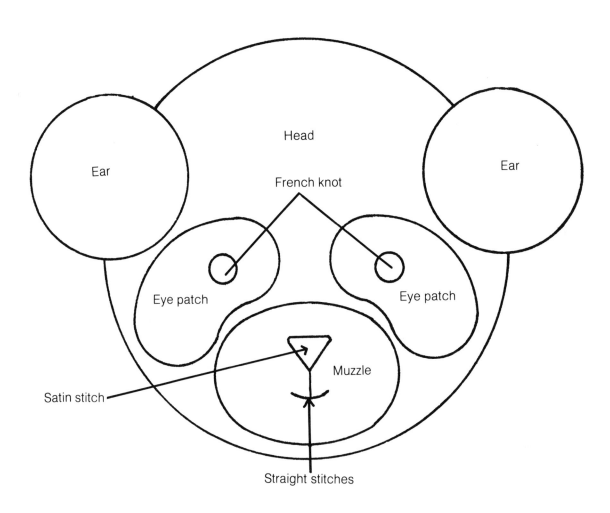

36 Baby's Bouquet

Approximate finished size: 30 by 41 inches

Yellow afghan-stitch strips provide the background for a large and lovely cross-stitched basket of violets to welcome baby, with tiny cross-stitched buds and ribbons worked along the outside edge. You might cross-stitch the baby's name and birthdate in the open center area of the blanket.

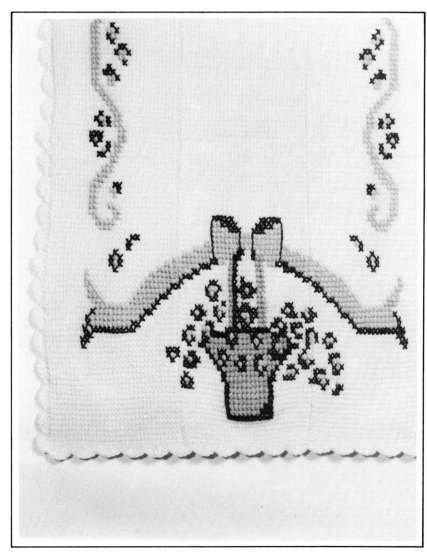

Materials:
Coats & Clark Red Heart Preference, 100-gram (3.5-ounce) skeins (knitting worsted weight)
    6 skeins color 231, yellow
Coats & Clark Red Heart Needlepoint and Crewel Yarn (3 strands, 12 yards)
    2 skeins color 652, light violet
    2 skeins color 642, dark violet
    1 skein color 466, tan
    1 skein color 205, rusticana (dark brown)
Afghan hook, size L
Crochet hook, size I
Yarn needle

Gauge: 7 stitches = 2 inches; 3 rows = 1 inch

Pattern Stitch:
Make a chain of specified length.
Row 1: First half: Ch 1, insert hook in second ch from hook, yo and draw through, *insert hook in next ch, yo and draw through, rep from * across. *Second half:* Yo and draw through first lp on hook, *yo and draw through 2 lps on hook, rep from * across.
Row 2: First half: Ch 1, skip first vertical bar, *insert hook from right to left under top strand of next vertical bar, yo and draw through, rep from * across, ending by inserting hook under both strands of last vertical bar, yo and draw through. *Second half:* Yo and draw through first lp on hook, *yo and draw through 2 lps on hook, rep from * across.
Rep Row 2 for pat st.

Strips: Make 3. With afghan hook and yellow, ch 34. Work even in pat st for 115 rows. Fasten off.

Finishing: With I hook and yellow, join the strips as follows: Place two strips side by side. Make a sl st on the hook and then, starting from the bottom, *insert the hook from right to left through the corresponding first vertical bars on the edge of each strip along the seamline, yo and draw through two vertical bars and through lp on hook, rep from *, working up the seam on each successive pair of sts along each side of seam and being careful not to pull sts too tight. When seam has been completed, fasten off and rep to join remaining strip.

Edging: *Rnd 1:* With I hook and yellow, join yarn in any corner and work in sc around entire joined piece, working 3 sc in each corner. Join with sl st to first st. *Rnd 2:* *Skip 2 sts, 5 dc in next st, skip 2 sts, sl st in next st, rep from * around, join with sl st to first st.

Embroidery: Work cross-stitch embroidery (see Stitch Glossary) in colors shown on chart. *Note:* The seamline sts each count as 1 st on chart.

☞ **Handwork Hints:** Although specific instructions are normally given for edgings, the number of stitches you work the edging over will not always be exactly the same as the multiple of sts that the edging instructions indicate so that you must use your judgment about how many slip stitches to make between scallops in order to make the edging extend along the stitches properly. For instance, on this blanket, if you reach the corner and find that you have two or three stitches to spare, simply slip stitch over them and start the first slip stitch of the next scallop on the first stitch after the corner.

Embroidery Chart

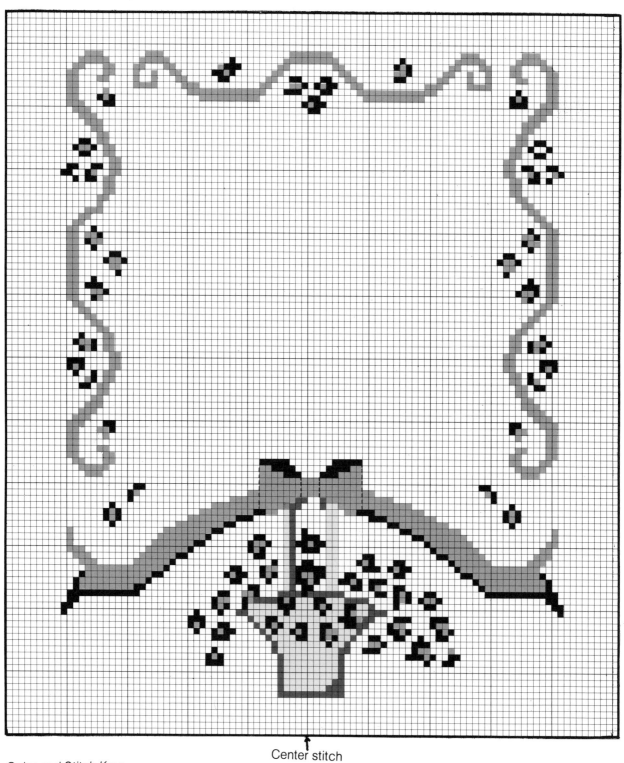

Center stitch

Color and Stitch Key:

■ Dark violet cross-stitch   ■ Light violet cross-stitch   ---- Dark violet stem stitch

■ Rusticana cross-stitch   ■ Tan cross-stitch   ▫ One stitch

144

Stitch Glossary

Crochet

Foundation Chain (ch)

Knot a slip loop onto the hook (A). Hold the hook in your right hand and place the long end of the yarn to be used over the index finger of the left hand, under the next two fingers, and lightly around the little finger. *Place the end of the hook under the length of yarn (this is called yarn over—yo), catch the yarn with the hook (B), and pull the yarn through the loop on the shaft of the hook. Repeat this process from the * as many times as specified in the directions.

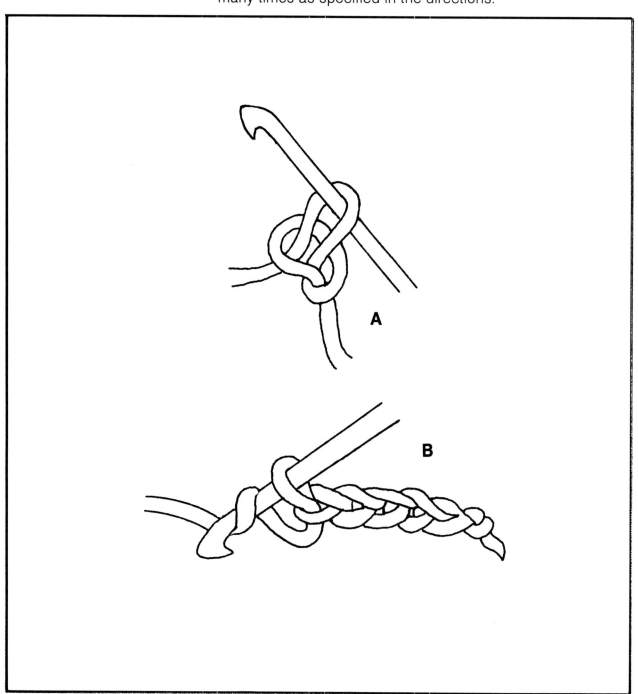

Slip Stitch (sl st)

Insert the hook under the two top strands of the stitch to be
worked, place the end of the hook under the yarn (this is
called yarn over—yo), catch the yarn with the hook, and pull
the yarn through the stitch and the loop on the hook in one
motion.

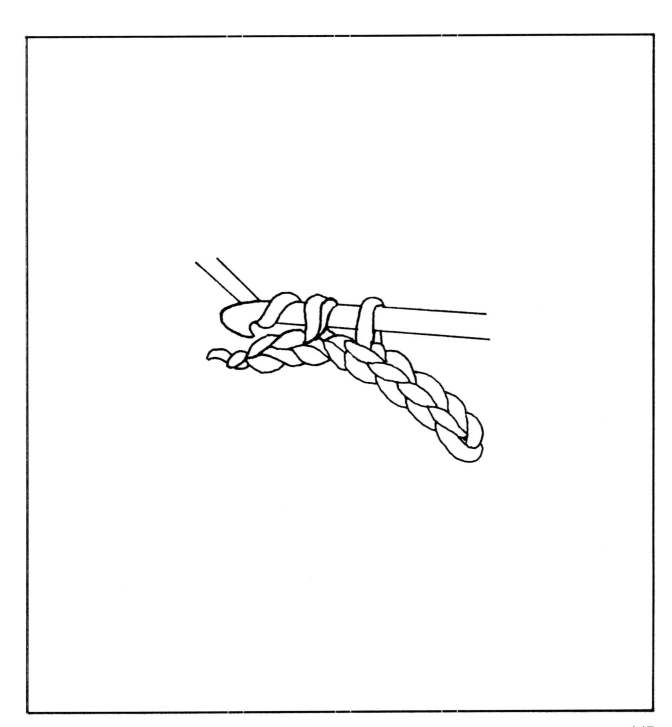

Single Crochet (sc)

Insert the hook under the two top strands of the stitch to be worked, place the end of the hook under the yarn (this is called yarn over—yo), catch the yarn with the hook, and pull the yarn through the stitch (two loops are now on the hook), yarn over and pull the yarn through the two loops on the hook.

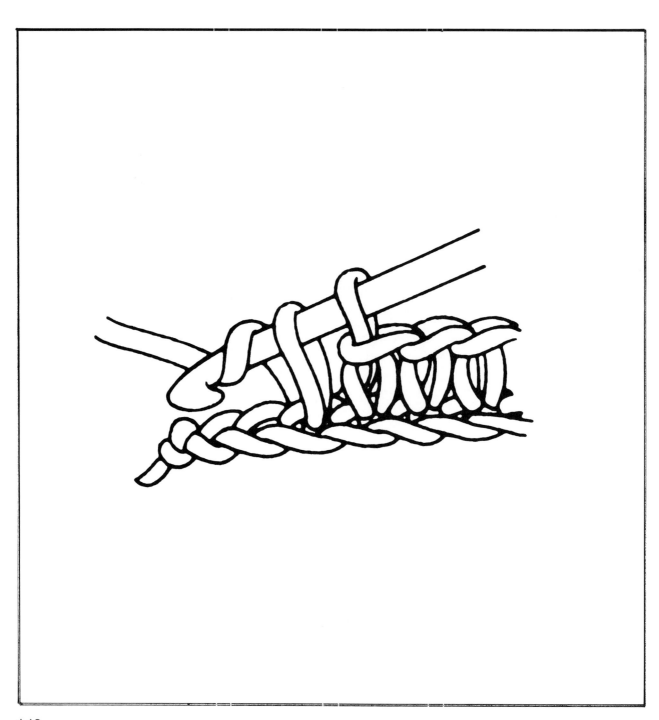

Half Double Crochet (hdc)

Place the end of the hook under the yarn (this is called yarn over—yo), insert the hook under the two top strands of the stitch to be worked, yarn over and pull the yarn through the stitch (three loops are now on the hook), yarn over and pull the yarn through all three loops on the hook in one motion.

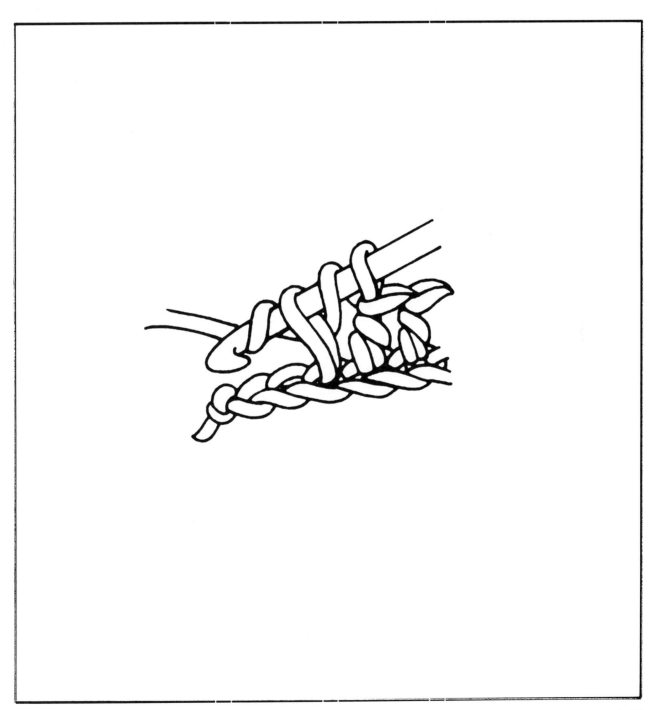

Double Crochet (dc)

Place the end of the hook under the yarn (this is called yarn over—yo), insert the hook under the two top strands of the stitch to be worked, yarn over and pull the yarn through the stitch (three loops are now on the hook), yarn over and pull the yarn through the first two loops on the hook, yarn over once more and pull the yarn through the remaining two loops on the hook.

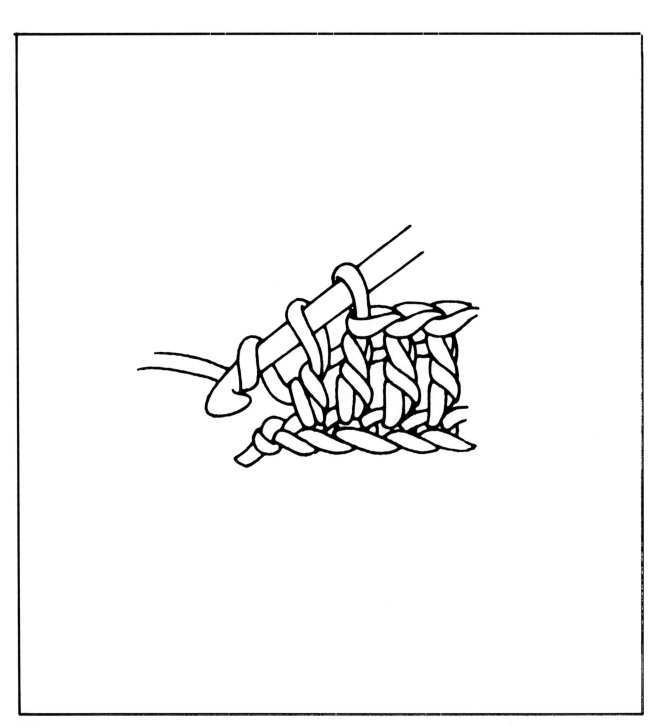

Treble Crochet (tr)

Place the end of the hook under the yarn (this is called yarn over—yo), yarn over once more and insert the hook under the two top strands of the stitch to be worked, yarn over and pull the yarn through the stitch (there are now four loops on the hook), yarn over and pull the yarn through the first two loops on the hook (three loops are now on the hook), yarn over again and pull the yarn through the next two loops on the hook (two loops are now on the hook), yarn over once more and pull the yarn through the last two loops on the hook.

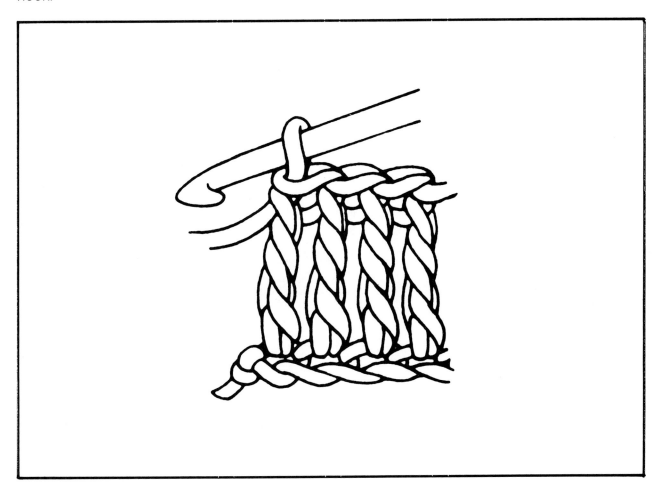

To Increase or Decrease (inc or dec)

In this book, the type of decrease or increase to be used, if any, is specified in the directions.

Knitting

To Cast On

Make a slip loop on your needle (A) about two yards (per 100 stitches to be cast on) from the end of the yarn. Hold the needle in your right hand with the two-yard end of the yarn closest to you, *make a loop around your left-hand thumb with the two-yard end and insert the needle from front to back through this loop (B). Wrap the yarn, extending from the skein or ball, under and around the needle (C). Pull the yarn, using the end of the needle, through the loop and pull the two-yard end down to tighten it around the needle (D). Repeat from * for the specified number of stitches.

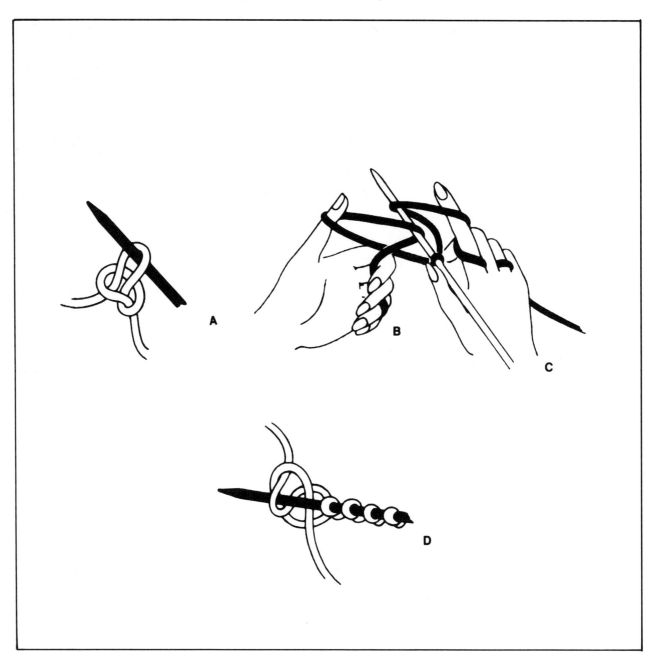

To Knit (k)

Hold the needle with the cast-on stitches in your left hand
with the yarn in back of the work, *insert the right needle from
left to right through the front of the first stitch, wrap the yarn
under and around the right needle to form a loop, pull the tip
of the right needle and the loop just made on it through the
stitch on the left needle toward the front, and then slip the
stitch just worked off the left needle; repeat from * across the
stitches on the left needle.

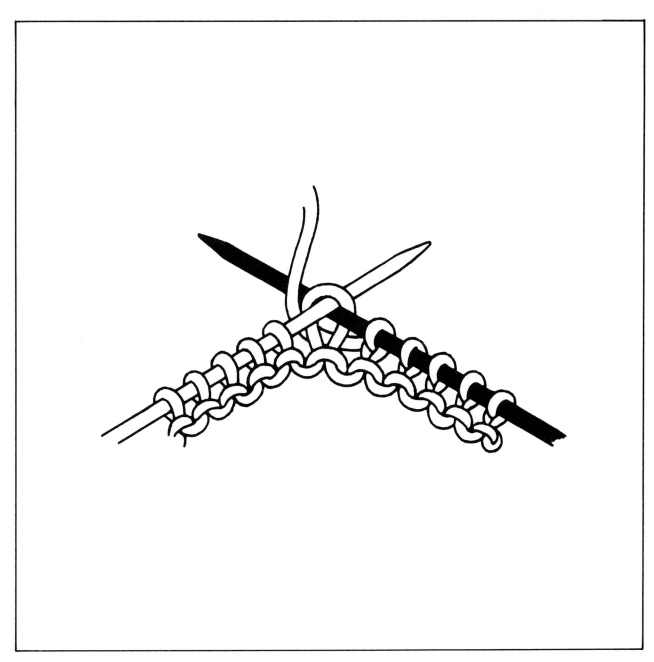

To Purl (p)

*Hold the yarn in front of the work, insert the right needle from right to left through the front of the first stitch on the left needle, wrap the yarn around the right needle to form a loop, pull the tip of the right needle and the loop just made through the stitch toward the back, and then slip the stitch just worked off the left-hand needle; repeat from * across the stitches on the left needle.

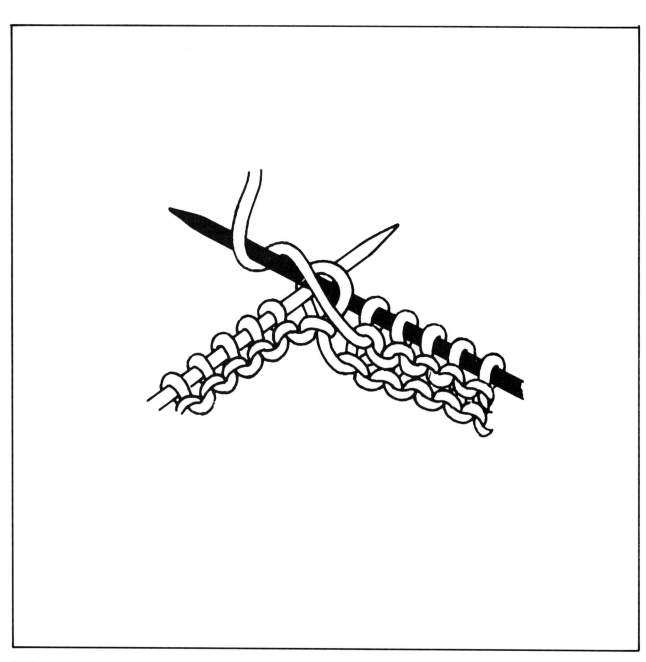

To Bind Off

Knit or purl, as specified, the first two stitches. Then *insert the point of the left needle into the first stitch on the right needle (A) and lift this stitch over the second stitch and off the right needle completely (B). Knit or purl the next stitch. Repeat from * for the number of stitches specified. When all the stitches are to be bound-off and you come to the point where there is only one stitch left, cut the yarn and draw the end of the yarn through the stitch.

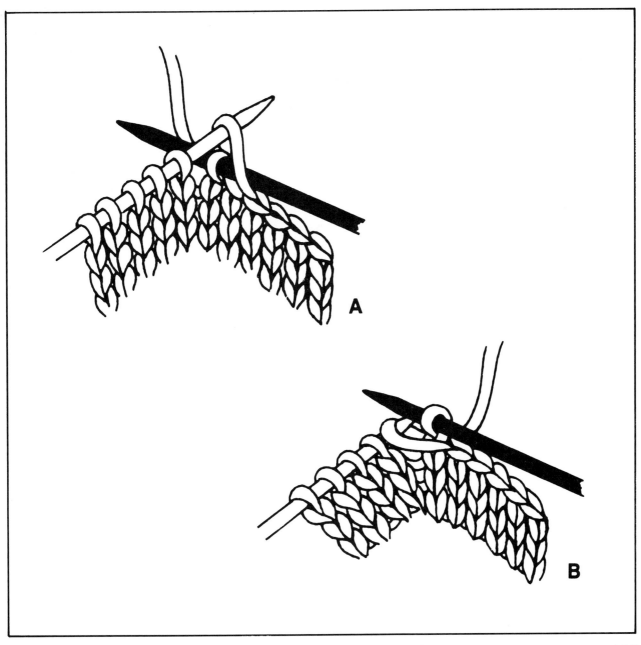

A

B

To Increase (inc)

When knitting, knit the stitch in which the increase is to be worked in the usual manner (A) and then work a knit stitch in the back loop of the same stitch (B). When purling, purl the stitch in the usual manner; then bring the yarn to the back of the work and work a knit stitch in the same front loop.

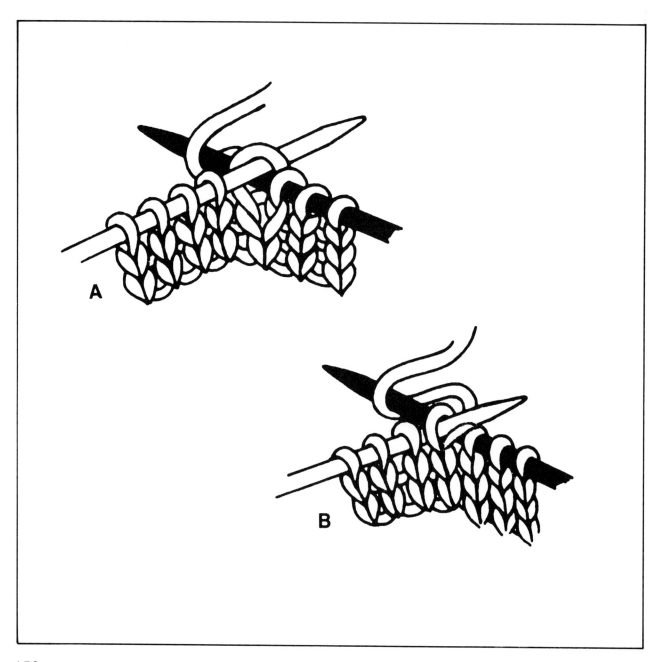

To Decrease (dec) or (k or p 2 tog)

Insert the right needle, either to purl or to knit as specified, through two stitches and work through these two stitches together as one.

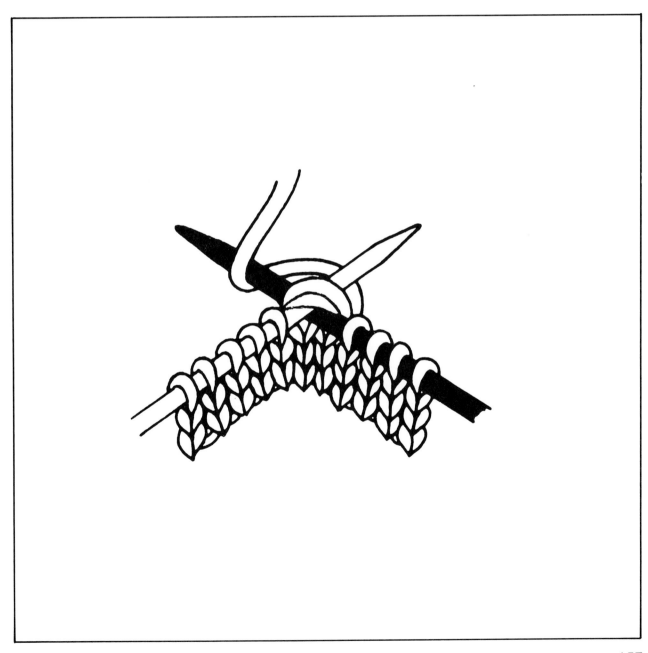

Slip Stitch (sl st) or (sl 1 as if to p)

Insert the right needle from right to left through the front of the stitch to be slipped and transfer it to the right needle without working it.

Pass Slip Stitch Over (psso)

Lift the slipped stitch on the right needle with the point of the left needle, pass it over the specified number of stitches and the tip of the right needle, and drop it.

Yarn over (yo)

To work a yarn over, wrap the yarn around the needle once, or as many times as specified, to create an additional loop on the right needle, which will be either knitted into on the next row to increase a stitch or dropped to create an elongated stitch.

Embroidery

Cross Stitch on Afghan Stitch

Each vertical bar of the afghan stitch counts as one stitch. Follow the desired diagram for the embroidery design. Join the thread or yarn on the wrong side of the work and bring the needle up through the small space to the lower left of the vertical bar. Then insert the needle down through the space to the upper right of the same vertical bar and then up, to the front, through the space directly below (A). When the specified number of stitches has been worked in this manner, complete the stitch by forming a cross from right to left (B).

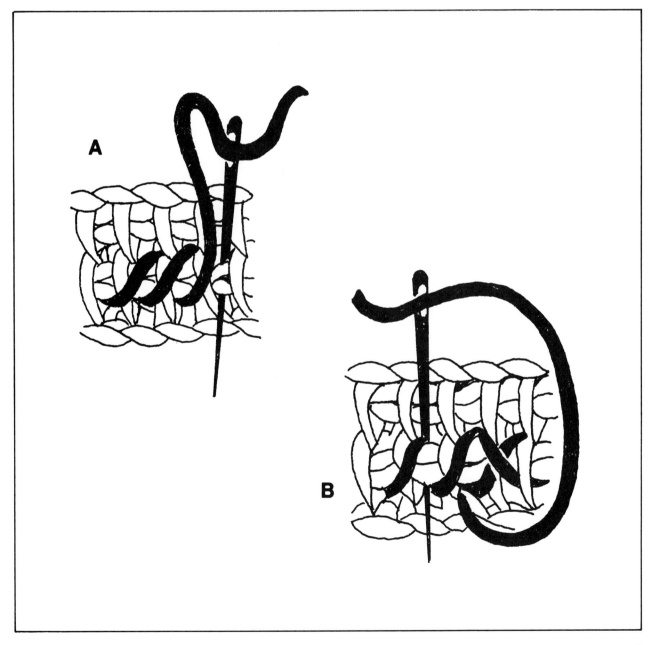

Duplicate Stitch

Following the desired chart for the design, bring yarn up, from wrong to right side, through the center of the base of a knit stitch. Insert the needle into the top of the right side of the same stitch and pass it through horizontally to the top of the left side of the same stitch. Insert the needle again into the center of the base of the stitch. Pull the yarn through with a light tension so that the yarn completely covers the stitch being embroidered.

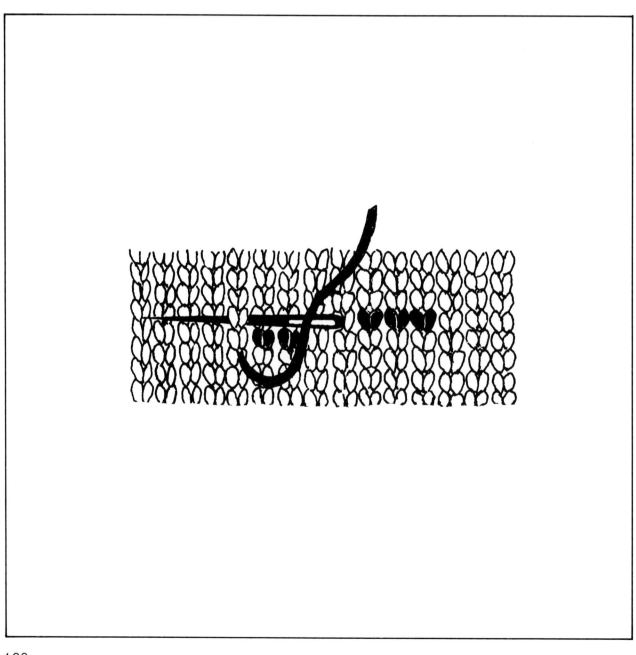

French Knot

Bring the thread or yarn through from the wrong to the right side of the work at point A and wrap it around the needle once or as many times as desired (1). Then insert the needle down through the work near point A (2). The completed stitch should look like Figure 3.

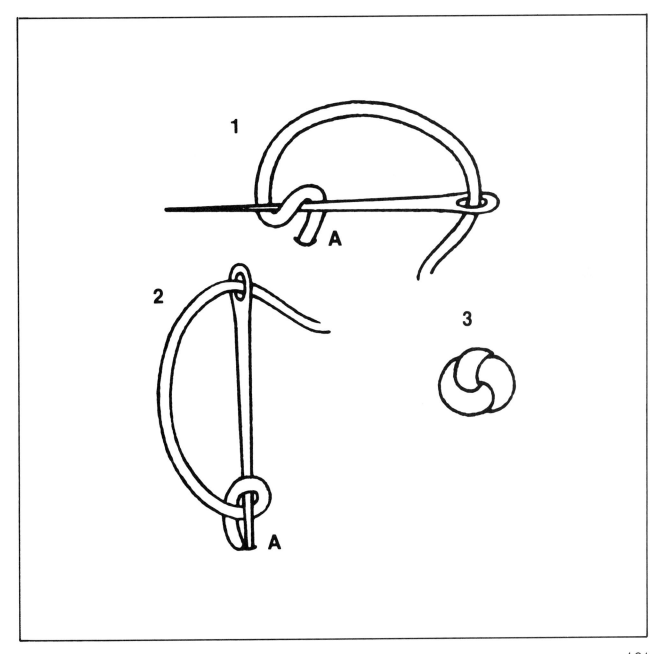

Long and Short Stitch

Work as for satin stitch (see next stitch explanation) but work the first row, following the outline of the shape to be filled, with alternating long and short stitches. The stitches in the following rows are worked in stitches of equal length but following the pattern established on the first row.

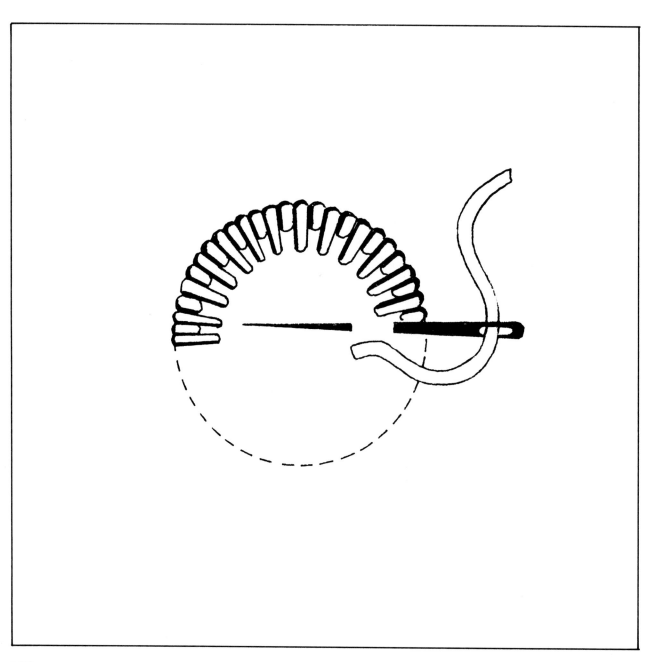

Satin Stitch

Bring the thread or yarn through at A along the outline of the
shape to be filled in. Insert the needle down through point B
at the opposite edge of the shape to be filled in. Carry the
needle across the back of the work and bring it out at the
point next to A. Continue to work in this manner until the
shape is filled in.

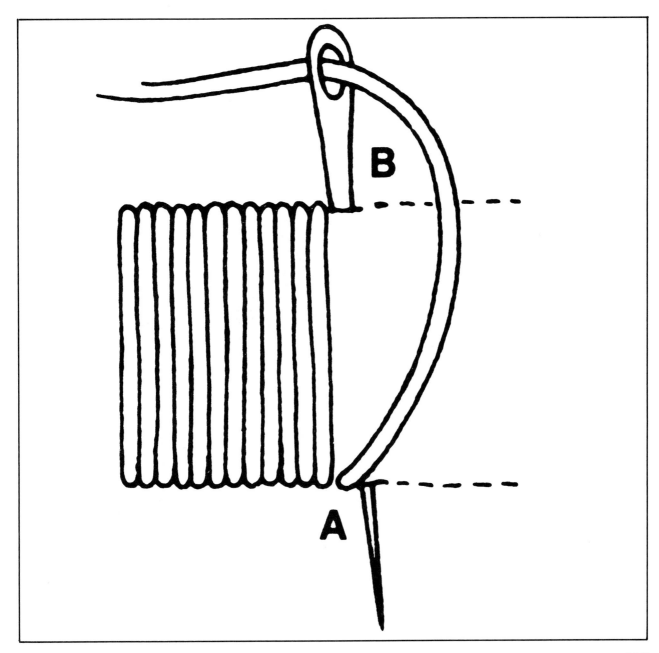

Stem Stitch

1. Bring the thread up at point A on the outline of the design and then pass the needle through the work from B to C. 2. Next, pass the needle through from D to B. 3. Continue working in this manner.

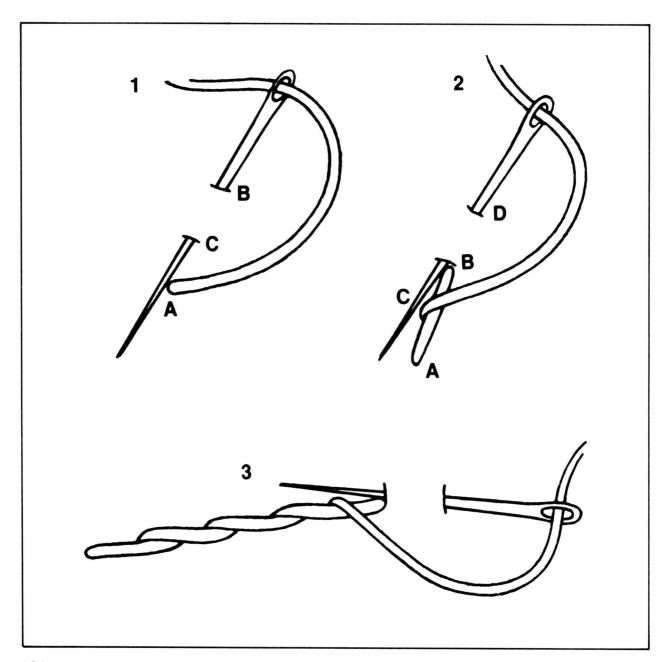

Straight Stitch

Bring the thread up through point A and insert the needle through the work at point B, following the design specified in the directions.

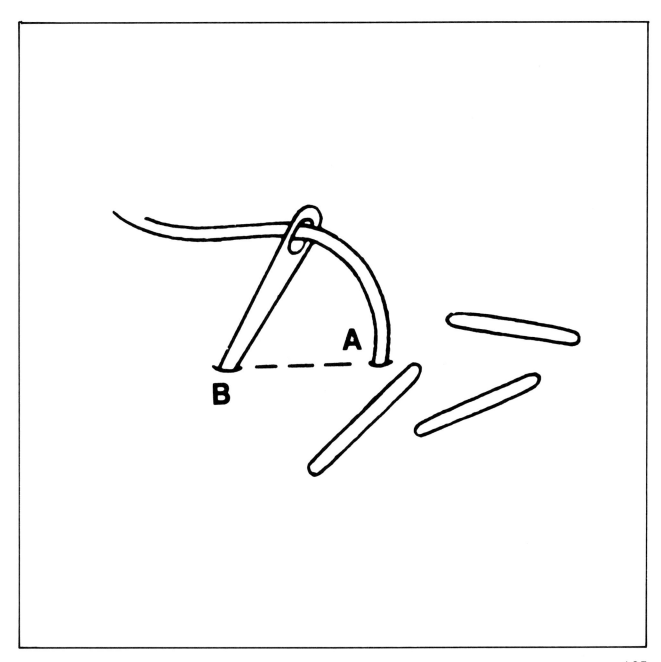

Running Back Stitch

Work from right to left. Hold the pieces together with right sides facing and work through both thicknesses. Bring thread up through point A, insert it at point B, and bring it out again at point C. Continue to work in this manner.

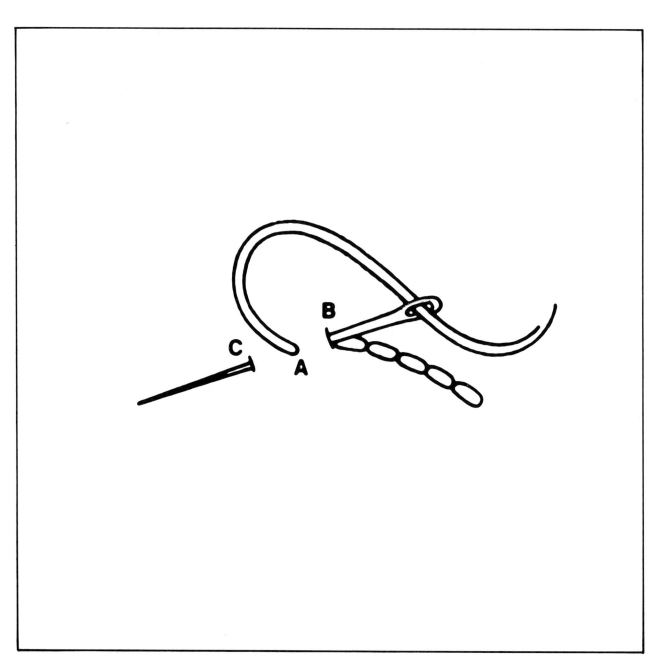

Joining Stitches

Overcast Stitch

Hold the two pieces edge to edge, matching them stitch for stitch, and bring the thread or yarn through both pieces in one motion, as shown.

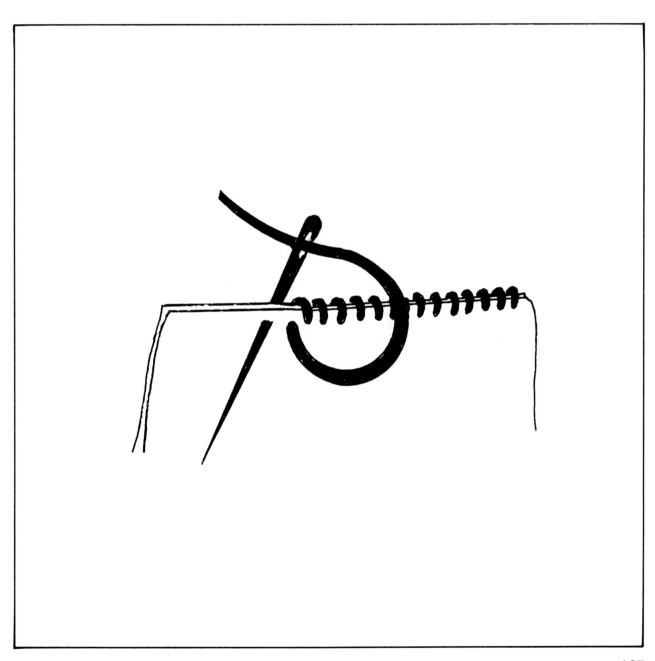

Index

Abbreviations, 17
All Points (3), 29-30
Argyle Borders (15), 58-60
Arrowtip Lace (14), 56-57

Baby Smocking (18), 70-72
Baby's Bouquet (36), 141-44
Berry Stitch Get-Together (22), 93-95
Binding off, 153
Blocking, 16, 34, 36, 50, 95
Blue Willow (29), 116-18
Bobbins, 59

Casting on, 150
Changing yarn colors, 27, 123
Chevron Stripes (11), 49-50
Circular needles, 64
Colonial Ripples (28), 114-15
Crayon Stripes (30), 119-20
Crochet stitches, 146
Crocheted edges, 15, 30
Cross-stitch on afghan stitch, 108, 159

Decreasing in crochet, 149
Decreasing in knitting, 155
Double crochet, 148
Duplicate stitch, 160

Edgings, 143
Embroidery stitches, 159
Enlarging a pattern, 117

Fan and Feather (6), 37-38
Fiesta (34), 134-36
Flowers at the Crossroads (23), 96-98
Flowing Lace (8), 42-43
Foundation chain, 146
French knots, 161
Fringing, 16

Gauge, 15
Grapevines (24), 99-101

Half double crochet, 148
Harlequin (10), 47-48

Icelandic Accent (7), 39-41
Increasing in crochet, 149
Increasing in knitting, 154
Irish Knit Updated (4), 31-34

Knitting, 151
Knitting stitches, 150

Lightning Strikes (25), 102-105
Log Cabin Quilt (2), 26-28
Long and short stitch, 162

Metric Conversion Chart, 17
Motifs Ahoy (27), 110-13

Navajo Symbols (31), 122-25
Neon Granny (19), 74-76

Overcast stitch, 167

Pandas on Parade (35), 137-40
Parrot (26), 106-109
Pass slip stitch over, 157
Patchwork Hearts (17), 66-69
Portable Lap Robe (32), 126-28
Practice swatches, 57
Purling, 152

Rattan (12), 51-52
Reading charts, 15, 21
Ribbons and Bows (16), 62-65
Running back stitch, 166

Satin stitch, 163
Seaming, 16, 38, 79, 98, 104
Seascape (1), 20-25
Simplified Instructions, 13, 17
Single crochet, 147
Slip stitch in crochet, 146
Slip stitch in knitting, 156
Snowflakes (9), 44-46
Squares in the Round (5), 35-36
Stem stitch, 164
Stitch Sampler (33), 129-32
Straight stitch, 165

Tension, 43
Tiny Blossoms (13), 54-55
Transferring embroidery designs, 55
Treble crochet, 149

Victorian Openwork (20), 77-80

Working color over color, 16
Woven Pastel Plaid (21), 89-92

Yarn, 14
Yarn over, 158